GREAT UNSOLVED MYSTERIES

GREAT UNSOLVED MYSTERIES

by James Purvis

Grosset & Dunlap
A Filmways Company
Publishers • New York

Copyright © 1978 by James Purvis
All rights reserved
Published simultaneously in Canada
Library of Congress catalog card number: 77-93956
ISBN 0-448-14630-4 (hardcover)
ISBN 0-448-14631-2 (paperback)
Printed in the United States of America
First printing 1978

Contents

Introduction

Every year thousands of people die or disappear under mysterious circumstances. Bodies are found too mutilated to identify. Healthy people expire for seemingly no reason. Apparently well-adjusted men and women walk out of their lives, never to be heard from again.

The vast majority of these cases involve little-known people in little-known situations. Only family and friends are concerned. The police make a routine investigation and the local paper may carry a small article. But despite the bizarre and tantalizing circumstances surrounding the event, it is lost to the general public. It becomes a statistic, a two-page report in a police book, and is buried forever.

In other cases the gruesomeness of the death, the notoriety of the victim, or the unusual method of death brings the case widespread publicity and as a result a major investigation is launched. Cast into nation-wide publicity many of these cases are apparently solved. The Patty Hearst abduction, the Son of Sam killings and the Lindbergh kidnapping are prime examples. Still others, however, pass even this scrutiny without solution. When this happens the world is left with a true Mystery.

These mysteries go back as far as recorded history. They range from the Man in the Iron Mask to Jack the Ripper. They have haunted every country and every time.

The twentieth century, has seen perhaps the most gruesome and bizarre Mysteries of all. Some are so macabre that beside them even the famed murders of Victorian England pale. Others are strange deaths in which both motive and method are shrouded in darkness.

And still others, which seem to be crimes, may in fact merely be enigmas, events we simply cannot explain.

This book is a collection of the most famous of these Mysteries. All are true. The pages that follow carry tales of violence and horror that will shock you. They are not for those with weak stomachs, and the pictures they paint are not pretty. But these are also incidents that challenge the powers of deduction and haunt the imagination. In each case some of the best minds of the times strove but failed to find an explanation. Thousands upon thousands of man-hours were spent in fruitless searching. Many of the investigations are still open.

If you are curious about life's mysteries, and if the possibility of imminent death that each day brings intrigues you, then read on. Some of the strangest stories you have ever heard await you.

GREAT UNSOLVED MYSTERIES

MASS MURDER

The Boston Strangler, the Son of Sam, Richard Speck, Charles Stark-weather . . . the list goes on and on. Each left a random trail of blood and terror in his wake. Each paid for his deeds. In the chapters that follow you will learn about another breed of mass killer, men who have caused equal amounts of bloodshed but who have paid no price for their crimes. No one knows who they are.

The Mad Butcher Of Kingsbury Run

IT IS A FALL AFTERNOON IN CLEVELAND, 1935. The leaves have fallen and there is a chill in the air. In the industrial valley that cuts through the heart of the grimy city, two young boys wander along a deserted gorge that serves to channel the city's railroad tracks out of the valley and on to Youngstown and Pittsburgh. The place is called Kingsbury Run and it is a favorite spot to search for the kind of throwaways and railroad junk that is so valuable to a child.

Playing tag and laughing the two boys run back and forth over the railroad tracks. Finally, they stop their game to take up some serious prospecting. As they move up the far edge of the Run, the younger lad comes across a small side ravine almost completely covered with weeds.

With a shout to his companion the boy starts to work his way into the undergrowth. It is virgin territory and he scans the ground eagerly. After a few yards the weeds thin out and abruptly he comes to a small clearing. He stops now and opens his mouth soundlessly in horror. For several seconds he can do nothing more than stare at the terrible sight. Then he screams, loudly, again and again. Seconds later the second boy is beside him. And he, too, is speechless.

Laid out in front of the boys are two naked male corpses. The bodies have no heads. The date is September 23 and although no one knows it yet, one of the most gruesome and mysterious mass murders in the history of America has begun.

Police arrived on the scene a short time later and even they were taken aback by what they found. The two men were laid out neatly side by side. There was no blood on the ground or in the bodies, indicating that the two were decapitated somewhere else, drained of blood, and washed up before being moved to Kingsbury Run. Both men's genitals were cut off.

A search of the immediate area by the police that day turned up a flashlight, a dipper, and a tin bucket. The bucket was full of a substance that later proved to be a mixture of oil, partly decomposed blood, and hair. A short distance away from the bucket the detectives found the missing genitals.

While the search was on, one observant policeman noticed some hair sticking out of the embankment on the other side of the gulley some fifty feet away. After the police had done careful tunneling, two heads rolled out. The detectives gingerly carried the gruesome objects to the decapitated bodies. The heads matched.

All the remains were then taken to the city morgue, where a careful autopsy was performed. The coroner quickly determined that one of the men was young, about twenty-eight, and had been dead for two or three days. The other man was about forty-five and very short and squat. He had been dead for at least five more days and the body had decomposed considerably.

What amazed the coroner most was the professional way in which the two men had been decapitated. Both cuts had been made just above the collar and the skin was cleanly cut. This meant someone had operated with skill and deliberation. The muscles in both necks had retracted, indicating that the heads were cut off while the victims were still alive or immediately after death while their reflexes were still operating.

Neither man had any other marks on his body except for some rope burns on the wrists of the younger victim.

Fingerprints from the younger body (the older body was too decayed to be identified despite extensive attempts) identified it as being the remains of a local tough named Edward Andrassy. Andrassy had an estranged wife and child, had worked for a while in a mental hospital. For the past several years he had eked out a living as a criminal in the streets of Cleveland's infamous Third Precinct. He was the kind that carried a knife and wasn't afraid to use it.

Digging into his shady past, police found that Andrassy also had a checkered sexual history. He had been seen in nightclubs with a variety of women but was also reported to have been seen picking up

16

Kingsbury Run victims Edward Andrassy and Florence Polillo—the only bodies ever identified. (UPI photo)

young boys. One specific incident, remarkable for its strangeness, demonstrates the extent of his unorthodox sexuality. The strangest story of all came from a married couple who had been unable to have a child. Andrassy accidentally learned about this, told the man that he was a "female" doctor, and asked to examine the woman. The husband agreed. During the examination, with the husband watching, Andrassy committed sodomy on the wife. Neither the man nor the woman complained.

The police searched Andrassy's room and questioned whatever acquaintances of his they could find. They also traced the items found at the scene of the crime. All the leads petered out, however, leaving the detectives with little more than a sordid history of the younger victim's past.

It was a frustrating investigation, but at the time it hardly seemed unusual. Cleveland in 1935 was a city full of European immigrants. The area immediately adjacent to Kingsbury Run, the Third Precinct, was a hotbed of competing nationalities, poverty, and crime. Many of these people were violent and feuds involving cruel murders were

17

commonplace. Under the circumstances the police filed away the Andrassy case, labeling it another local vendetta.

Although, as a matter of police record, this was the official beginning of what would subsequently prove to be a long series of murders, another incident which in fact preceded it should also be mentioned. A year before Andrassy became the victim in the Kingsbury Run killings, a man walking on Lake Erie beach near Cleveland's amusement park (near the city limits) found part of a woman's torso—the lower trunk and thighs—buried in the sand. Several days later the upper part of the torso was found farther down the beach. The head, the arms, and the lower legs were never found. Police were unable to identify the body from what was left and the case was closed.

Four months after Andrassy's body was discovered, the next victim turned up in the roaring Third Precinct itself. On January 26, 1936, a local butcher investigating a report of "some meat in a basket" in a nearby alley found two thighs, a right arm, and a lower torso. The parts had been wrapped in newspaper, placed in half-bushel baskets, covered with burlap bags, and placed against the outside back wall of a factory.

The coroner was able to identify the parts of the body as belonging to a middle-aged woman, short and heavy set, with dark brown hair. As in the previous cases, all cuts had been neatly made. The amputated limbs had all been detached cleanly through the joints, using only a sharp knife.

Twelve days later the rest of the body, except for the head, was found scattered behind a vacant house a short distance away. Tests proved that these parts had been left there the same day the first parts had been left in the alley. Once again all the cutting was precise. The muscles around the neck were retracted, indicating as in the first murders, that the victim had been decapitated alive.

Fingerprints from the one hand available quickly identified the victim as a thirty-six-year-old local prostitute and drifter named Florence Polillo. When the police delved into her background they found it as anonymous and ugly as Andrassy's. Flo lived alone in a cheap boarding house and drank heavily. She had drifted through a variety of men, many of whom had beaten her up. She had been arrested for prostitution twice and was well known in the speakeasies and whorehouses in the area. In her room she kept a neatly arranged collection of dolls.

Once again the detectives tackled every lead they had. They questioned all of the people known to associate with Flo. They tried to trace the burlap bags and the bushel baskets. Although they came up with a mysterious man who fit a description in the Andrassy case, they never really got anywhere. Whoever had committed the murders had been very skillful or very lucky in covering his trail (in the Andrassy case this was no small trick as it involved lugging around two fully grown male bodies. Down at Homicide, the detectives on the investigation read and reread the numerous reports they had compiled on the two identified victims, hoping to uncover some clue they had missed earlier, but they found nothing. All that their months of digging had provided was a pile of inconclusive facts. Little did the police know that what they had, sparse as it was, was more than they would ever get again.

On the morning of June 6, 1936, two schoolboys headed down Kingsbury Run towards Lake Erie. It was a beautiful day and the two were playing hookey. As they walked down the valley along the railroad tracks, one of them noticed a pair of pants rolled up underneath a tree on the embankment. Feeling playful, the boys grabbed a long stick and poked at the pants. To their horror, a head rolled out and bounced down to their feet. Victim number five had been discovered.

The head was that of a handsome young man with fine sensitive features. When police searched the area they found a pair of shoes and socks lined up neatly near the pants.

The following day, in a weeded area, farther down between two sets of tracks, the rest of the body was found intact. There were no marks on it or signs of a struggle. Only the clean incision in the middle of the neck revealed the violence of the death.

Police were unable to find the man's fingerprints on record, but at first they were hopeful that they could identify him through the six tattoos on his body, including three with names or initials. Tattoo parlors around the city were investigated. The first night, some two thousand people were brought to the morgue to see the victim. Photos of the body were circulated around the Third Precinct. They even tried putting a plaster cast of the face on display at the Cleveland Exposition during the summers of 1936 and 1937. A massive effort was made, but despite all this the authorities never determined the man's identity.

Theories were batted around and grimness began to pervade the Homicide Bureau. As part of the new focus, a search of Kingsbury Run was carried out. The search was fruitless.

Victim number six was found a short time later on the other side of town. For the first time it appeared that the murder had been carried out on the spot. The male body was nude but the clothes were found nearby. Nothing in the clothing gave the police anything to go on. The coroner established that this victim had been dead some time and had actually been killed before the tattooed man. Fingerprinting was impossible and the name of the victim was never discovered.

This was the only body found on the West Side of town and it prompted a lot of theories, all of them, of course, speculative. Was the victim a hobo that the killer had chanced upon? Was he just another victim that the killer had lured to the West Side for personal reasons? Was the killer scouting new sites? No one will ever know.

Six weeks later the police had a new body to investigate and even less to go on. The latest victim (number seven) was found in a deep, stagnant pool that had formed where several sewers empty before entering the Cuyahoga River. On September 10, a hobo waiting to hop a freight saw two halves of a man's torso floating in this rancid body of water.

Police using grappling hooks managed to bring up the lower legs and thighs. Then a diver went into the fetid water. Finally, the police drained the entire pool. Despite all this, the arms and head were never found. Nor were the genitals. This victim, like the first two, had been castrated.

By this time, police had mounted a citywide investigation. It was obvious to all that the murders were the work of one man. The case was baffling. There were no signs of rage in the killing, nor was the sexual angle clear cut (only three of the corpses had been sexually abused and the victims were of both sexes). Some of the bodies had been dismembered to facilitate disposal, but others had been moved intact with great difficulty. In short, the police could make out no clear-cut motive or consistent method of operation.

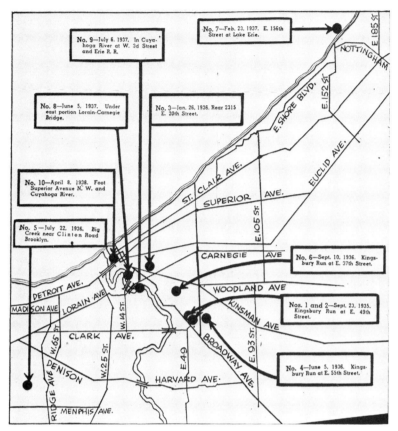

No. 7—Feb. 23, 1937. E. 156th Street at Lake Erie.

No. 9—July 6, 1937. In Cuyahoga River at W. 3d Street and Erie R. R.

No. 8—June 5, 1937. Under east portion Lorain-Carnegie Bridge.

No. 3—Jan. 26, 1936. Rear 2315 E. 20th Street.

No. 10—April 8, 1938. Foot Superior Avenue N. W. and Cuyahoga River.

No. 5—July 22, 1936. Big Creek near Clinton Road Brooklyn.

No. 6—Sept. 10, 1936. Kingsbury Run at E. 37th Street.

Nos. 1 and 2—Sept. 23, 1935. Kingsbury Run at E. 49th Street.

No. 4—June 5, 1936. Kingsbury Run at E. 55th Street.

The Mad Butcher's death-strewn trail across Cleveland.   (UPI photo)

By now the murders had created something of a sensation in Cleveland. Despite the fact that all the victims had been from among the poorer element of the city, the staggering brutality of the crimes had horrified everyone. Downtown shopping fell off and middle-class women venturing anywhere near the Third Precinct did so with trepidation. Railroad workers began to look over their shoulders as they moved cars around in the yards. Track inspectors, frequent visitors to the Run, began to work in teams. Perhaps most significantly of all, the numerous hobo camps that dotted the area in those Depression days all but disappeared.

Citizens began to inundate the police with all kinds of tips and rumors. A quickly augmented force of detectives found itself investigating every sort of strange and demented character in the city. Escaped mental patients turned up, along with drug addicts and sadists. One detective even came across a man known as the Chicken Freak, an otherwise normal citizen who was seen frequenting houses of prostitution carrying a live hen under each arm.

Despite this massive inquiry, nothing substantial turned up. All that the police were able to determine was the following: the man probably lived near the Run; he was at least somewhat knowledgeable about anatomy or butchering (as, for example a hospital orderly or a hunter might have been); he performed the butchery in a room in the area; he got to know his victims before killing them; and, most importantly, the murderer was not recognizably insane. He was very clever and calculating about what he did and probably led a very normal life apart from the killings.

About this time, police in New Castle, Pennsylvania, reported that during the last ten years they had found thirteen nude, headless bodies in a swamp near their city. New Castle lies on a rail line that connects with Cleveland. City police went over to take a look, but, despite the similarity in style, there was no positive evidence to link the crimes.

Corpse number eight showed up in Cleveland on February 23, 1937. In this case the upper half of a woman's torso was found on the beach very close to the same amusement park where the earlier body (the one discovered before the official start of the case) had been found. Two months later the other half of the torso was seen floating in the lake not far from the mouth of the Cuyahoga River. Once again, all the amputations were cleanly done. There were dirt and weeds in the flesh, suggesting that the body had lain on the ground for a while before being dumped in the water. The arms, legs, and head were never discovered. Many speculated that the cut-up parts of the body had been thrown in the river and had then floated out into the lake.

At 5:30 A.M. on June 6, 1937, the bridge tender on the Third Street Bridge spotted something floating slowly down the oily Cuyahoga River. Moving out to the middle of the bridge he was finally able to make out the lower half of a man's torso. During the next eight days all the other parts of the body floated by except for the head. The only thing unusual about this victim number nine were the incisions, some of which appeared rough, almost angry.

Nine months later, number ten, a woman, started down the river just as number nine had. Finally, on August 16, 1938, the corpses of numbers eleven and twelve were found at a lakeside dump. Both were badly decomposed and were in the usual condition.

These last bodies set off a new public outcry that was even larger than the previous one. People began to speak of "the Butcher's Dozen." Newspapers demanded action from the police and local officials were flooded with calls, letters, and telegrams from outraged citizens.

The police responded by launching an even bigger investigation. Additional detectives were assigned to the case. Old files were re-worked. Every lead, no matter how inconsequential it seemed, was followed to the end. But once again, the inquiries yielded absolutely nothing. After twelve gruesome murders and nearly three years of investigation, the authorities were no closer to solving the crimes than they had been at the beginning.

No one knows what stopped the killing. Maybe it was the enormous publicity and frantic police work. Maybe it was a remission of whatever strange psychotic urge had driven the killer. Maybe he died in a traffic accident. Whatever the reason, the killings stopped with victim twelve. Slowly but surely a kind of peace returned to the Third Precinct. The daily struggle to live continued, but gradually railroad workers stopped looking over their shoulders and bridge operators began to gaze at the waters of the river without apprehension.

Active investigation continued for several years and the case was kept officially open long after that. To this day there are police force old-timers who still wonder about the identity of the killer.

Time has done little to help solve the mystery of the killer's identity. Conjecture is still virtually all that is possible. Even the officials closest to the case disagreed violently on what kind of man the killer might be. The coroner felt he was a person "of more than average intelligence. He probably originated from a higher stratum of society."

The detective who headed the investigation saw the murderer as both sexually degenerate and uneducated. In his view, the man (a female identity was suspected for a while, then discarded) was a habitué of the hobo camps and traveled along the train routes of the day.

This detective spent an inordinate amount of his own time on this case and even continued his work after he retired. He remained convinced not only of the general identity of the killer, but also that he never really stopped, but instead just moved. The detective points out in a very frightening manner, that after the Butcher's Dozen was over, similar killings continued elsewhere. The same year as the murder of the last of the twelve, another decapitated body was found in New Castle, Pennsylvania. The following spring, three more were found in boxcars just outside Pittsburgh. In 1942 two more were found in the same city. Still other headless bodies were found as far west as California.

Did the Mad Butcher of Kingsbury Run die, did he lose his murderous urge, or did he move on to safer hunting grounds? Who was he? Was he a doctor gone mad or a sadistic criminal with a lifetime of underworld activities? No one will ever know.

The Axeman Of New Orleans

JAKE MAGGIO LAY SILENTLY on his bed and tried to gather his thoughts. A faint light was beginning to show through the window and Jake guessed it to be nearly five A.M. For a second the young man blinked rapidly, trying to understand why he had awakened so early.

Then the groans came again. They were accompanied by a rasping, gurgling sound that made Jake's hair stand on end. There was a moment of silence and then the sounds were heard once more. Suddenly realizing that they were coming from his brother and sister-in-law's room on the other side of the wall, Jake jumped up and roused his older brother, Andrew. Together they rushed out into the hall and flung open the adjacent bedroom door. What they saw stopped them in their tracks.

Their sister-in-law lay sprawled on the floor in a mass of blood. Her head had been badly bludgeoned and her throat was split from side to side, almost completely decapitating her.

Their brother , Joseph, lay back on the bed. His head, too, was badly beaten and his throat was slit, but by some miracle he was still alive. It was from him and his bloody throat that the horrible moans and gurgling sounds had come.

When Joseph saw his brothers he tried to get up and half fell out of the bed. Jake and Andrew called the police at once and set about doing what they could.

The Maggios both owned and lived over a small grocery store and when the police arrived they found a panel of the door had been chiseled out. A blood-soaked axe was discovered outside on the back steps. The razor that had been used to slash the throats was found near the bodies.

The year was 1918 and the place was New Orleans. The infamous Axeman had struck. In the months to follow his terrible exploits would turn the Mardi Gras city upside down, terrorize the Italian community, baffle police, and create a mystery that lingers to this day.

The police investigating the attack that early summer day seemed hopelessly confused from the start. The major portion of their initial efforts was spent questioning the neighbors. Acting on a spurious tip that Andrew had come home late that night, the police on the scene promptly arrested the two brothers and charged them with murder.

A short time later a message was found chalked on the sidewalk near the house of death. It said, "Mrs. Maggio is going to sit up tonight just like Mrs. Tony." Detectives in homicide quickly recalled that in 1911 there had been three axe murder cases, all strikingly similar to the Maggio crime. In all three, the victims had been Italian grocers and their wives. In the last case the victim's name had been Tony.

The next day an embarrassed police department released Jake and Andrew. They had been revealed to be hard-working, honest men. And it had also been shown that on that fateful night Andrew had been returning from a party to celebrate his draft call. Several people were available to testify that he was too drunk to attack anyone, much less his beloved brother.

The newspapers gave a lot of play to the crime, but as weeks passed and no new developments occurred, interest in it waned. The Great War was reaching its bloody climax and the terrible stories coming from the Continent quickly eclipsed the murder in the public mind.

Then, in the early morning of June 28, a local baker making his deliveries arrived at the grocery store of Louis Besumer. Finding the store still closed, the baker went around to the back to leave the fresh bread. To his horror he found a panel of the back door chiseled out. Remembering the Maggio crime and terrified that the killer might be inside he knocked timidly. The baker jumped a mile when the door opened almost immediately.

Instead of the killer, however, the baker was confronted by Louis

Besumer, his face pale and shocked, blood streaming from a deep wound on his head.

The baker rushed into the house and found Mrs. Besumer lying unconscious on the bed. She, too, was covered in blood and had a terrible gash in her skull. An axe was found, in the bathroom still glistening red.

Both attack victims survived and Louis was released from the hospital the next day. He was no sooner back on his feet, though, when he became engulfed in some rather strange developments. The local newspapers had discovered that he was Polish and had only recently come to New Orleans from South America. It was also learned that he spoke several languages fluently and that he regularly received letters from abroad. With that the local papers began a campaign of innuendo, implying that Besumer might be a spy for the Kaiser. When approached by the papers Louis quickly denied being a spy or a killer. He said he was innocent, a victim himself, and that he was Polish and not German, for God's sake!

Further difficulties were created by Besumer's statement that he was not married to the woman he had been living with. She did not recover consciousness until July 5. By that time she had been identified as Mrs. Harriet Lowe. Almost as soon as she was able to talk and hear what was going on, Mrs. Lowe gave a statement. "I've long suspected that Mr. Besumer was a German spy," she said. Louis was quickly arrested.

The next day Harriet gave another statement. "I did not say Mr. Besumer was a German spy. That is perfectly ridiculous." Louis was released.

A few days later Harriet started talking about the attack. She described the assailant as a stranger, yet the specific information she gave out started everyone thinking of Louis as a spy again. A war fever gripped the city and Mr. Besumer became a very unpopular man.

A month later Harriet passed away after surgery. She died mumbling that Louis had hit her with the axe. Louis went back to jail.

The harassed police were very happy to finally have a murder suspect firmly under lock and key (Harriet now being unable to change her story). The same night that Louis was arrested, however, the Axeman struck again.

The new victim was the young pregnant wife of Edward Schneider. Schneider returned home late that night and was horrified to find his bride lying on their bed, unconscious, in a pool of blood.

The Schneiders were lucky. Mrs. Schneider recovered completely and was able to give birth to a healthy child.

Police questioned her closely but all she could remember was opening her eyes, seeing a dark form standing over her with an axe, and seeing the weapon come down at her. Combining her descriptions with those of Louis and Harriet, police came up with a description of a rather tall, heavyset white man. There was nothing else to go on.

The latest attack set the local papers off on a new track. The day after the Schneider assault the *Times-Picayune* carried a large type headline: "IS AN AXEMAN AT LARGE IN NEW ORLEANS?" The city didn't have to wait long to find out.

On August 10, four days after the headline, Joseph Romano was attacked in his bedroom. The attack was interrupted by a young niece, who got a brief glimpse of the Axeman as he fled. Romano staggered out to the living room and managed to walk to the ambulance, but two days later he died from the massive wounds he had received.

Once again a door panel was found chiseled out. Once again the bloody axe was found in the backyard. Once again nothing was stolen. A pattern had been established. The only difference in this case was Romano's profession. He was a barber.

A wave of hysteria began to sweep the Italian community, especially among the grocers. Dark rumors of Mafia activities began to circulate. Families began to set up night watches, making sure that someone in the household was awake all night. Other families left the city.

As the newspapers picked up the cry, the hysteria swept to other parts of the metropolis. The police began receiving all sorts of reports about the Axeman. Several Italian grocers claimed to have had their door panels chiseled out, or to have seen a man with an axe in or near their home. Others claimed to have seen a man with an axe fleeing through their backyards.

As the police began to feel public pressure, they turned back to the only suspect they had, poor Louis Besumer. The general attitude seemed to be that no matter what else had happened, or whether he was guilty of any of it, Louis killed Harriet and we're going to make him pay.

In March of 1919 the Axeman struck again. The latest victims were a family of Italian grocers named Cortimiglia. On the evening of March 10, Iorlando Jordano, another Italian grocer living across the street, heard screams coming from the Cortimiglia house. He rushed over, followed by his younger brother, Frank. Inside they found Charles Cortimiglia lying on the floor, his body covered with gaping wounds. Mrs. Rosie Cortimiglia sat in the middle of the floor clutching the bloody body of her two-year-old daughter. Mrs. Cortimigilia was hysterical and refused to let anyone take her dead daughter from her. When the police arrived, they found all the now too-familiar signs: the chiseled door panel, the bloody axe, and the absence of theft. Both Charles and Rosie survived.

When Rosie was able to talk she described the attack in detail. She said she awakened to see her husband struggling with a large white man, armed with an axe. After a long struggle the intruder broke free and delivered a brutal blow with the axe that dropped her husband to the floor. With that the Axeman swung around towards Rosie.

Rosie said she promptly grabbed her daughter, who was asleep in a nearby crib, and hugged her to her breast, screaming, "Not my baby! Not my baby!" The Axeman swung twice, fatally hitting the baby and wounding Mrs. Cortimiglia.

A few days later Charles recovered enough to leave the hospital. No sooner was he out than Rosie changed her story. To everybody's amazement she began to accuse the Jordanos (who owned a competing grocery store in the same block) of committing the murder.

The police immediately questioned her husband. He was incredulous. No, the Jordanos didn't do it. Yes, they came in to rescue us. Despite this very strange testimony the police proceeded to arrest the Jordanos.

The elder Jordano, who was sixty-nine and in poor health, protested his innocence, citing the unlikelihood of his being able to commit the crime. It was quickly shown that the younger Jordano, who was a big man, could hardly have squeezed through the door panel. Shortly after the arrest Rosie was released from the hospital.

She proceeded to the jail where, in front of the press, she screamed at the Jordanos and fainted.

The Jordanos were scheduled for trial in May. Before the authorities could attempt to convict them, however, they had to try Louis Besumer, who was still waiting in another jail cell. Louis went on trial on April 30. The trial was very short and the prosecution looked rather foolish. Federal agents admitted they had no evidence whatsoever of espionage. Police accusations and testimony became very shaky on the stand. Flat statements given out to the press earlier turned out to be hearsay and rumor. Louis was acquitted.

By now all of New Orleans had been caught up in an "Axeman Craze." The papers played up every sensational angle and every man in the street had a theory. "Axeman" parties were held and a local songwriter turned out a tune entitled "The Mysterious Axeman's Jazz."

On March 14, a letter signed "The Axeman" was received by the *Times-Picayune*. In the letter he said he planned to visit New Orleans on the night of March 19 and added that he loved jazz and would pass by any house playing it. When the nineteenth came the noise was incredible. Bars and nightclubs were packed and residential streets echoed with the sounds of thousands upon thousands of record players blaring out jazz at full volume.

In May the Jordanos went on trial. The courtroom was packed and the whole thing got intensive play in the media. Witness after witness took the stand, but only Rosie's testimony suggested the Jordanos were guilty. Charles (now separated from his wife) got on the stand and vehemently denied that the Jordanos had been involved. Despite this the jury somehow found the Jordanos guilty and sentenced Frank to hang.

A few months later the Axeman went back to work. On the evening of August 10 an Italian grocer named Frank Genusa answered a knock at his door. He opened it to have his friend and fellow grocer Steve Boca fall into his arms. Boca's skull was cleaved open and he was covered with blood.

Boca recovered enough to talk the next day. Police searched his home and found all the usual signs. Following what was now appearing to be normal police procedure in New Orleans, they arrested

Genusa for the murder. Boca himself cleared his friend and the cops turned back to their fruitless investigation.

Three weeks later the Axeman struck at the home of a druggist but was scared away when the man fired a revolver through the door.

The next day a nineteen-year-old-girl was found badly beaten and unconscious in her bed. No door panel was missing (the intruder came in through a window) but an axe was found outside.

On October 27 of that year the Axeman made a deadly appearance at the home of Mike Pepitone, still another Italian grocer. Mrs. Pepitone surprised the attacker in the bedroom with her husband just after the attack had occurred. Mike was dead and his blood covered the walls and ceiling. The Axeman fled as Mrs. Pepitone began screaming. Once again the police were left with only a very general description of the killer.

It was at this point that Rosie Cortimigilia rushed into the city room of the *Times-Picayune* and demanded to see a reporter. She was highly emotional. Thin and gaunt she hardly seemed the same person who had appeared in court. Throwing herself on her knees in front of the reporter who listened to her, Rosie screamed, "I lied! I lied! God forgive me, I lied!" A few days later the Jordanos were freed.

By now the citizens of New Orleans, especially the Italian citizens, had given themselves up to fear. The police had proven worse than useless in catching the killer and the Axeman seemed insatiable.

But just at that moment, when everything seemed hopeless, the attacks stopped. Mike Pepitone was the last person to fall under the killer's axe. There was no sign, no word to indicate why the attacks stopped. The police doggedly continued their investigation but virtually nothing was turned up. Only one incident provides any possible solution to the mystery.

About the time of Rosie Cortimiglia's confession, a New Orleanian named Joseph Mumfre was shot dead in Los Angeles. He had been walking down the street when a veiled woman dressed in black stepped out and emptied a revolver into his body. The woman made no attempt to flee and was promptly arrested. She turned out to be Mrs. Mike Pepitone. She told police she had seen Mumfre in her husband's bedroom and traced him to Los Angeles. She said he was the Axeman.

Mrs. Pepitone pleaded guilty in court. There was a lot of public support for her and she was sentenced to ten years in jail. She was freed after three.

The New Orleans police had Mumfre on file. He had a long jail record and the dates when he had been locked up dovetailed perfectly with the gaps in the Axeman's activity. Despite this the police refused to accept Mumfre as the killer and left the case open. The consensus of public opinion also held that the mass murderer's identity had not been discovered. The newspapers held the same view.

Many people feel that there was more than one Axeman. Some still insist the Mafia was responsible. Others speak of a vendetta against Italian grocers. The answers now are jumbled and worn with time. Whoever the Axeman really was will remain a secret forever.

Zodiac—The Sign of Death

IT WAS JUST A FEW DAYS before Christmas, 1968, and the roundish hills outside Vallejo, just north of San Francisco, were covered with a thin layer of white frost. Moonlight flooded the scene and gave the entire area a ghostlike whiteness. But this stark beauty went unnoticed by the young couple parked on lonely Lake Herman Road. David Faraday, seventeen, and Bettilou Jansen, sixteen, were on their first date. Nervous and excited over the possibilities of romance they had eyes only for each other.

Suddenly a lone figure approached the car. Crouching by the driver's window the now visible man pulled out a 22-caliber pistol and aimed it at young David's head. A shot rang out, and then another, and then another. Inside the car, blood spurted from David's head. Across the seat Bettilou screamed. After a moment's hesitation, she yanked the door open and began to run frantically. But she was not fast enough and five more bullets brought her to the ground. It was all over in minutes. An innocent young couple lay dead, the only clue to their murder the nine shell casings spread around the area.

Police investigating the murders leaned towards jealousy as the motive. Fellow students and friends of the couple were hauled in and interrogated. The police got nowhere because the Lake Herman Road killings were not isolated slayings. The motive was not personal jealousy. The Zodiac Killer was at work. He would be heard from again.

Interest in the double killing died as the investigation petered out. Over the spring and into the summer, the area around Vallejo returned to normal. Then, on July 4, Zodiac struck again. This time the victims were a twenty-two-year-old Vallejo waitress and a nineteen-year-old friend. That fateful night the two were parked alone in nearby Blue Rock Springs Park. Again the two were so deeply involved with each other that they missed the approach of the lone figure. For the first time there was a moment of warning, however short and useless. Turning a strong flashlight on the young man, the killer blinded and immobilized him for a brief moment before filling the interior of the car with bullets. This time Zodiac employed a powerful 9-millimeter handgun. Ten shots smashed through the car. Then the deadly figure turned and fled.

The waitress died a short time later but the young man miraculously survived the four bullet wounds and lived to give a sketchy description of his assailant. Blinded by the light, he remembered only that the man was fairly heavy and wore glasses.

A short time later, the Vallejo Police Department received an anonymous phone call. A man spoke very matter-of-factly. "I just shot the two kids at the public park. With a 9-millimeter automatic. I also killed those two kids Christmas." The caller hung up and the hunt was on.

The case gained even more notoriety when, on August 1, letters from the killer showed up simultaneously at the Vallejo newspaper and at both major San Francisco dailies. Each message contained a handwritten note and one-third of a cryptogram. The cryptogram was a mysterious series of letters and signs that defied easy interpretation.

As a means of establishing his identity in the note, the killer gave several details of the killing not known to the public. He listed the brand of bullets used and described the positions of the bodies. He also described the clothing worn by one of the female victims.

The note had several misspellings (possibly deliberate, as the complexity of the cryptogram certainly indicated the killer was a man of some intelligence) and closed with a warning. If the newspapers didn't publish the encoded message for all to see, the murderer would go on a killing spree. The note was signed with what would soon become known as his symbol, a circle divided by a cross.

The papers published the cryptogram and the note along with a message to the killer asking for more proof of his identity. As publicity

Bryan Hartnell and Cecelia Shepard had their picnic cut short by the Zodiac Killer. Hartnell lived to tell about it despite multiple stab wounds in the back. (UPI photo)

was undoubtedly part of the killer's motivation, he responded quickly. The *San Francisco Examiner* soon received a letter with still more details of the crimes. This time the killer gave himself a symbolic name as well as a symbolic signature. "This is Zodiac speaking," the letter began. Headlines were born.

The authorities expended a good deal of effort in attempts to crack the encoded message. In his last letter Zodiac had stated that when the police solved the cryptogram they would be able to catch him. A variety of experts were called in and the message was even fed into a computer. Nothing worked.

Finally two amateurs in Salinas (a high school teacher and his wife who had never tried to break a code before) were piqued by what they read in the newspaper. They tackled the job on their own and succeeded. The message they decoded sent chills through their hearts. "I like killing people because it is more fun than killing wild

35

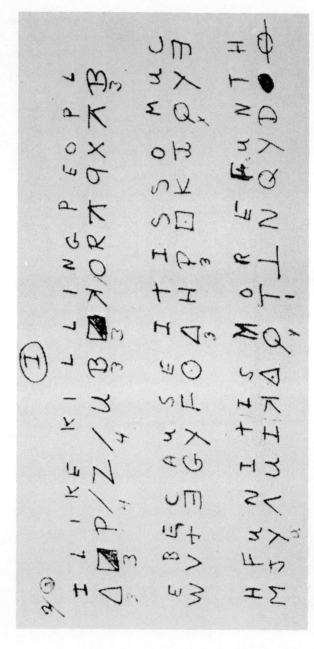

One of the Zodiac killer's cryptograms. Amateurs broke the code after the Navy failed.   (UPI photo)

game in the forrest because man is the moat dangerus anamal of all to kill something gives me the most thrilling expeerence.

"The best part of it ia thae when I die I will be reborn in paradice and all the I have killed will become my slaves. I will not give you my name because you will trs to sloi down or stop my collecting of slaves for my afterlife."

The message gave no solid clue to Zodiac's identity but it did give some insight into his motives. Sexual inadequacy, said more than one psychiatrist after reading the decoded statement.

Despite intensive investigative efforts by police, nothing new in the case happened until Zodiac struck again. This time the victims were two college students picnicking north of the city. Now Zodiac approached in broad daylight. Hiding his face with a square hood reminiscent of a medieval executioner's mask, he pulled a gun on the terrified young people and tied them up with a rope. Once they were helpless, Zodiac pulled out a long, sharp knife and plunged it into the man's back. He struck five more times before turning on the young woman. While he was stabbing her in the back, she turned over convulsively. The mad killer then proceeded to stab her in the torso twenty-three more times, the wounds forming the outline of a bloody cross.

Afterwards Zodiac walked over to the couple's white sports car and wrote on it the dates of all the murders he had committed. Amazingly enough, the young man survived despite his severe injuries. Because of the hood, however, there was little new information that he could give police.

Thirteen days later Zodiac killed again, this time inside the city of San Francisco itself. A cab driver, a part-time student working on his Ph.D., was the new victim. Zodiac hailed the cab and shot the driver from a backseat near a playground in Presidio Heights. When he finished his grisly work, he tore a piece out of the man's now bloody shirt and fled on foot. This time, however, there was a witness. Unbeknownst to Zodiac, the crime and his flight had been observed.

A short time later, police circulated a description of a man twenty to twenty-five, with a reddish crew cut and thick glasses. Armed with the description, police finally began to hope for an arrest. Working backwards through all of the data in the Zodiac case, they attempted to pin down a suspect fitting the new profile. They were unsuccessful,

WANTED

SAN FRANCISCO POLICE DEPARTMENT

NO. 90-69   WANTED FOR MURDER   OCTOBER 18, 1969

ORIGINAL DRAWING   AMENDED DRAWING

Supplementing our Bulletin 87-69 of October 13, 1969. Additional information has developed the above amended drawing of murder suspect known as "ZODIAC".

WMA, 35-45 Years, approximately 5'8", Heavy Build, Short Brown Hair, possibly with Red Tint, Wears Glasses. Armed with 9 MM Automatic.

Available for comparison: Slugs, Casings, Latents, Handwriting.

ANY INFORMATION:
Inspectors Armstrong & Toschi
Homicide Detail   THOMAS J. CAHILL
CASE NO. 696314   CHIEF OF POLICE

The closest the police ever got to identifying Zodiac.   (UPI photo)

although they did manage to come up with details of an earlier murder that they now attributed to Zodiac.

By this time the entire city and its suburbs were in a state of terror. The killer had struck randomly in different areas and at different kinds of people. Nobody felt safe. Women and men alike began looking over their shoulders. Public outcry for an arrest reached epic proportions.

A few days after the cab murder Zodiac heightened the sense of panic by writing a letter in which he stated that a school bus might be his next target. He just might shoot out the front tires, he said, and pop off the kiddies as they came bouncing out. Whatever Zodiac's intentions were, this last letter moved the city to a siege mentality. Police escorts were assigned to school buses and many parents either kept their children at home or took them to school in cars.

But Zodiac never struck at a school bus. In fact he never struck again. In the months that followed he sent a steady stream of letters to the newspapers, either taking credit for some new murder or twitting the police for failing to capture him. Each lead was checked out but either no evidence of a murder could be found or the guilt for it was indisputably attached to someone else. As the letters continued to arrive and as they began to embody little more than the Zodiac's perverted sense of humor, the newspapers began to bury them on the back pages.

In March of 1971 Zodiac wrote his last letter. Nothing has been heard from or about him since. Despite a massive police hunt that involved forces all across the Bay area, despite nationwide publicity and appeals for help, and despite an aroused citizenry armed with a description, very little is known about Zodiac. The police theorize that he is either in a hospital or dead. Others think he may be in jail, serving time for some relatively innocuous offense.

Still another possibility haunts the Bay area. The Zodiac may be neither dead, nor jailed, nor hospitalized. He may be walking the streets of San Francisco, his murderous urges under control for the moment. He may be the model of a normal citizen on the outside, but a walking time bomb inside, a killer in suspension waiting for some hidden impulse to drive him on to new mass murders.

Jack The Stripper

WHEN THE SUBJECT of famous unsolved crimes is brought up, one case always comes to mind. Jack the Ripper, the notorious nineteenth-century murderer, is possibly the most well-known criminal of all time. In the ninety years since he wreaked terror on London, countless policemen, newspaper reporters, scientists, and writers have pored over the few facts known about him in an attempt to discover who he was. Scores of books have been written both in England and the U.S., many of them proposing complex theories about his identity. Little known to the general public, however, is the existence of another London criminal whose infamous exploits were far more deadly than those of Jack the Ripper. This unknown man, like his nineteenth-century counterpart, preyed exclusively on prostitutes. But going the Whitechapel killer one better, the 1965 monster stripped his victims naked and removed some of their teeth. As in the 1888 killings, all the bodies were found in the same general area. Because there were so many similarities between the two sets of murders, it was perhaps inevitable that the newspapers dubbed the modern-day killer, Jack the Stripper.

The first "London Nude" victim was pretty Hannah Tailford. Her body was found floating in the Thames on February 2, 1964, not far from a secluded area (Duke's Meadow) often used by prostitutes and young couples. The body was naked except for nylons that had been rolled down around her ankles. All her other clothes were missing except for her panties, which had been stuffed into her mouth, apparently to keep her from screaming.

Hannah was known to the police. She had a wild background

and "specialized" in group parties. More than one of these episodes had been filmed and the authorities first speculated that she might have been killed in a blackmail attempt. Such things had happened before.

The police launched a regular homicide investigation into her death and talked to more than seven hundred people. They established little more than the details of her sordid past and the fact that she was last seen nine days before her death. Only one unusual fact emerged. She was pregnant at the time of the murder.

The second victim was discovered on April 8, floating in the river right at the edge of Duke's Meadow. Like Hannah, Irene Lockwood had been stripped before being dumped in the water. No underpants had been stuffed in her mouth, however. There was no need, she had been strangled.

Again as with Hannah, the police initially speculated that Irene might have been killed during a blackmail attempt. It was known that Irene (who was identified by a tattoo on her arm reading "John in Memory") had run with another prostitute who had been murdered for precisely this reason.

While the authorities pursued this angle, a man stepped forward and announced that he was the culprit. Because the man was able to give several precise details about the second victim, the police charged him and sent him to trial. Unfortunately for them, Jack the Stripper struck again during the trial and the man was acquitted, returning to his lonely life after a brief moment in the limelight.

The latest victim provided the police with their first real leads. Number three was an ex-convent-girl-turned-prostitute named Helen. Like the first two, Helen had been strangled and stripped. Unlike the others, however, she was found on land (in an alley) and it was obvious that her clothes had been removed after death. Four of her front teeth were missing and most importantly of all, flakes of spray paint were found on her torso. A quick lab test showed that after death her body had been kept in or near some establishment that used spray paint.

It wasn't much to go on but it was all the authorities had. They now realized they were facing a truly mad killer and only an all-out effort might be able to stop him from killing again. A major search was launched for a spray-paint establishment that would fit the crime.

At the same time Scotland Yard, taking a highly unorthodox step, went to the public and asked for help in tracking down the killer.

The majority of the calls received in answer to the appeal dealt with one or another of London's thousands of pimps and whores, but produced little in the way of solid clues. The publicity, did, however, apparently scare the Stripper. For nearly three months he stayed home. The lull lasted until July 14.

Victim number four was found propped up against a garage door in a suburban area. In this case the murderer came close to revealing his identity. Once again the woman had been strangled and then stripped. And once again several of her front teeth had been removed. (Police began to speculate that the killer engaged in oral necrophilia.) More importantly, a few moments after the body was discovered by a local resident, another neighbor approaching in a car was narrowly missed by a van tearing away from the scene. Unfortunately for the authorities, the neighbor didn't have a chance to catch sight of the license plate.

Once again police were left without a solid clue to go on. Background checks of the girl and her associates turned up little. Attempts to trace her movements during the preceding twenty-four hours were also unproductive. By now all of London was aroused by the killings. Women alone on the streets were visibly nervous about strange men. Fear reigned among the thousands of streetwalkers. Abuse and occasional violence are part of the game for prostitutes, but the emergence of a truly vengeful killer is making them his prey ignites the flame of terror as nothing else can. Even the toughest whore has difficulty in seeing the hidden violence in a madman's heart.

Victim number five turned up under a pile of rubbish in a parking lot on November 25. The body had been dead for over a month and it was so badly decayed that police had to cut the hands off to obtain fingerprints. These and tattoos that read "Helen, Mum and Dad," identified the victim as a Scottish prostitute named Margaret McGowan. Many people in England remembered Margaret because she had been involved in the Profumo scandal and had testified in court.

Once again the police launched a major effort to develop some sort of lead. The victims had to have something in common, detectives reasoned, and they searched hard to find it. Once again they

Jack the Stripper's fifth victim and a figure in the Profumo Scandal. (UPI photo)

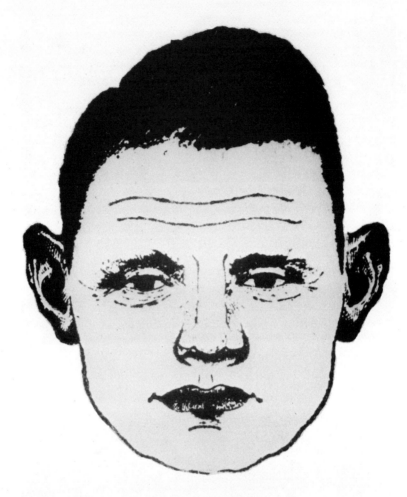

A police sketch of the mass killer who terrorized London.   (UPI photo)

struck out. Tracing Margaret's illicit activities brought a variety of people into view, but clearly none of them was the Stripper.

The last victim was discovered behind a building on a large estate-turned-housing development called Heron Trading Estate. Her name was Birdie O'Hara. Like the other victims Birdie was a woman of the streets and like the other victims she had been strangled and stripped before having several of her front teeth removed.

Birdie's death, however, gave the police new information; for the first time they had real hope that they might find the killer. The body had been partially preserved in death, indicating that until the time of her discovery, she had been kept indoors somewhere in a very unusual environment. As with the body of Helen, specks of spray paint were found indicating that Birdie, too, had been kept in a small room near a painting establishment. There were also bits of oil on her that seemed to point to her body having been near some kind of machinery.

The public outcry over the case had reached huge proportions by this point and Scotland Yard reacted by assigning its top detective, Chief Superintendent John Du Rose, to head an expanded investigation.

Du Rose began by marking off the entire western section of London where the crimes had occurred and sending massive numbers of detectives out to track down every conceivable garage, workshop, and factory that might have held the body. At the same time, regular police began checking on every vehicle in the area that was in any way suspicious. Du Rose also escalated the amount of publicity given the case and indicated that he was coming steadily closer to nailing The Stripper.

The intensive police investigation paid off a short time later when a building that housed a transformer was discovered to be the storage place for both Birdie's and Helen's bodies. The transformer was located on the same Heron Trading Estate and was located close to a spray-paint shop. Everything now indicated someone in the immediate neighborhood and the dozens of detective teams assigned to the case were concentrated in the closely surrounding areas. Despite the new evidence, Scotland Yard's finest were in the end unable to uncover the killer. For a while it appeared that they had temporarily at least succeeded in scaring him off, but soon it became evident that he had stopped altogether.

In an effort to finally unravel the mystery, Du Rose began a massive search through all the suicides, accidental deaths, and jailings in London since the last murder. Sifting through the thousands of records that were forwarded by different agencies, Du Rose finally came up with a suspect who fit the crimes. The man had been a security officer in the area and had been on duty at the time of each crime. He committed suicide shortly after Birdie's body was found and left a note saying he couldn't take it anymore. He was a family man and his wife and children were totally bewildered by his death. Despite these incriminating facts, a thorough search of his personal belongings turned up nothing to link him to the crime. Nevertheless, the authorities indicated that they were satisfied that Jack the Stripper was dead, but others were not then nor are they now so sure. While it is entirely possible that the suicide was indeed the killer, other facts make it quite possible that he was not. Like the Cleveland Butcher and the Zodiac Killer, Jack the Stripper may well have managed to repress his murderous urges for a while. Disguised as a normal person he may well be leading an average, everyday life today somewhere in London. Is Jack the Stripper really dead? Or is he merely "out of work." No one may ever know . . . unless he strikes again.

A TOUCH
OF THE MAFIA

The tentacles of organized crime reach out into all parts of our lives. Death and silence are their twin marks. Who knows what events they have twisted and what lives they have taken . . .

The Harry Oakes Murder

THE SQUAT, HEAVY SET BODY lay sprawled on its back, one arm dangling over the side of the bed. Dried blood caked much of the head and neck. Large sections of flesh were burned away about the face and along the limbs. The blackened skin matched the color of the burned mattress under the body and the few remaining sections of mosquito netting. There was a lingering odor of burned flesh on the gentle Caribbean breeze. As a final, macabre touch feathers had been spread over the dead man's body.

A variety of people crowded about the bed and filled the room, either searching for clues or just gawking. There was a growing sense of excitement among those there, for the body on the bed belonged to Sir Harry Oakes, in 1943, the Bahamas' number-one citizen. The grotesqueness of the death scene and the prominence of the victim were enough to ensure a certain notoriety, but some of the people there felt there was more to the story. They were right. The mystery of how Sir Harry Oakes died would shake this Crown colony with a scandal that would ultimately touch not only the dead man and the tranquility of the islands, but also the Miami police department, Meyer Lansky, and the Duke of Windsor himself. A tale of intrigue, corruption, and human weakness would unfold that would rival a Hollywood movie. In the end the events would be clouded with uncertainty and mystery, for despite the wide publicity and the notoriety of the people involved, the crime would never be solved.

In 1943 being the most important citizen of the Bahamas meant a great deal more than it does today. Sir Harry Oakes held that distinction by force of money, a lot of money. When he died, he was

51

considered to be one of the richest men in the world. Rumor had it he could write a check for $200 million and cash it.

A native of Maine, Oakes was born to middle-class parents. He was moody and had been a loner from childhood. In his second year of law school he dropped out and went to the Klondike (with his family's approval) to prospect for gold. It was his destiny, he said, to amass great wealth during his lifetime. For the next fourteen years he wandered around the world, penniless, seeking instant wealth from mining. His visits carried him to Australia, Death Valley, the Belgian Congo, and a hundred other places in between. Finally he found himself in Ontario, and through luck or skill (the truth is unclear) developed the Lake Shore Mines, the yield of which in time made his discovery the second largest gold strike in history.

Harry Oakes, who in the meantime had become a naturalized Canadian, overnight became its richest citizen as well. He prospered there until the Canadian revenue service caught up with him. Outraged at what he considered unfair restrictions (Harry was used to getting his way, instantly), he decided to change his nationality again.

In the early 1930s he met and befriended Harold Christie, a Bahamian "entrepreneur" who was to become the Bahamas' second citizen. Informed that these islands had no income tax at all, Harry moved there lock, stock, and barrel (although he still maintained houses in Canada, Maine, Palm Beach, London, and Sussex) and promptly bought up approximately one-third of his new homeland. In no time at all, he had busied himself in local activities and was *the* man to see about business ventures.

Eventually Harry decided to become a baronet. By spending the right money in England he changed his name to Sir Harry. A more far-fetched person to be a nobleman could hardly be found. Fourteen years of prospecting in some of the wildest places on earth had destroyed him almost every particle of social grace. Unlimited wealth and power had squashed any refinement that was left. Sir Harry ate beans with a knife. He spit seeds and pits out wherever and whenever he felt like it. Tact was unknown and undesired. In short, except for his money, he wouldn't have been allowed in the front door of the local hotel.

Early in 1943 according to some sources, Harold Christie approached Sir Harry with a new scheme. Christie had supposedly

Sir Harry Oakes in better days.   (UPI photo)

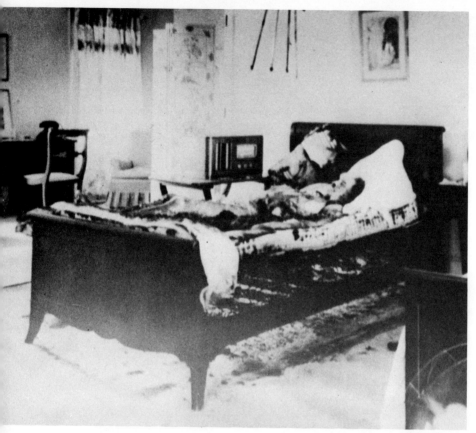

The burned body of Sir Harry as it was found in the morning. (UPI photo)

been in contact with up-and-coming mobster Meyer Lansky, who had offered to build and run a casino in the Bahamas in return for exclusive gambling rights on the islands. Lansky had offered to sweeten the deal by throwing in a million dollars as a "gift." Christie foresaw a fortune and convinced Sir Harry to go along with the deal, to expedite a local ordinance that had to be passed. One other man had to be in on the scheme to ensure its success, and that was the royal governor, who in 1943 was none other than the Duke of Windsor, the recently abdicated King of England. No one knows

54

what Christie said to the duke but he apparently gained his consent rather easily.

The "sweet little deal" fell apart when Sir Harry suddenly had second thoughts and reneged on the agreement, withdrawing his approval. At this point the stage was set for one of history's finest little mystery melodramas.

Sir Harry's body was discovered by Harold Christie early on the morning of July 8. The duke was awakened with the news at 7 A.M. For three hours and fifty minutes he remained in his quarters with his wife. It took no great intelligence to realize that the casino deal might have something to do with the crime.

Finally the duke put in a call to Captain Melchen of the Miami police department. Melchen had provided the bodyguard for him on one of his visits to that city. The duke asked Melchen to come to the Bahamas immediately to confirm the details of the suicide of a leading citizen. At the same time, he ordered that news coverage of the event be censored. Unfortunately for him, Harold Christie had made enough hysterical phone calls to ensure worldwide coverage of the murder.

Captain Melchen, accompanied by fellow Miami policeman Captain Barker, arrived in the afternoon and immediately began one of the most lackadaisical criminal investigations of modern times.

The local police were pushed completely out of the picture. But nobody else was. Anybody that cared to was free to wander over the Westbourne mansion, where the body was found, and touch whatever they liked. A few fingerprints were taken and a few people interrogated but the investigation was by no means comprehensive.

It was soon obvious to the American policemen that it was out of the question to label the death a suicide. Sir Harry had died of massive head wounds inflicted with some sort of a pronged instrument. Then the bed was set on fire and Sir Harry's body was incinerated. Then the feathers had been spread on top. Hardly self-inflicted wounds!

Hurried conferences were held between the two Americans and Christie, and eventually the duke. Late on the second day the Americans declared a breakthrough. They said they had a suspect and promptly sent the local police out to arrest him. The man they arrested was Alfred de Marigny, Sir Harry's son-in-law.

De Marigny made a perfect suspect. Sir Harry had openly hated him, and believed him to be conniving after his father-in-law's wealth. Alfred had a reputation as a playboy. He had been divorced twice, and was alleged to have had a close friend who followed him around and ended up sharing both his wives. To top it all off, because he was from the island of Mauritius in the Indian Ocean, everybody in the Bahamas considered him an "outsider." He was decidedly unpopular.

Despite his questionable character, Sir Harry's young daughter, Nancy, was quite devoted to her husband. This had caused a major rupture in the Oakes household as Alfred was *persona non grata* around her father. When Alfred was arrested, Nancy believed implicitly in his innocence. Arrangements were shortly made for a top-flight island barrister to defend him and for a famous American private investigator to aid the barrister with the case. The investigator's name was Raymond Schindler. When he arrived on the island he found the atmosphere so hostile and the apparent cover-up so complete that he was able to accomplish almost nothing. When he arrived at the murder mansion, he found police scrubbing down the walls and in so doing erasing several bloody handprints. Although he protested, the police refused to stop, saying, "The prints aren't those of de Marigny, therefore they'll only confuse the evidence."

Wherever Schindler went on the island he was followed by police. Whenever he interviewed a witness, the police reinterviewed them. His telephone appeared to be tapped. The authorities obviously had their orders, and these orders were to prevent a thorough investigation.

The trial began some thirteen weeks after the crime. The murder was front-page news by this time and correspondents from all over the world were in attendance. Famous writers such as Erle Stanley Gardner were among them.

On the islands the trial was a social event of major proportions and wealthy landowners sent their servants to queue up for seats long before dawn.

The prosecution's case was fairly standard. De Marigny was a man of ill repute who wanted his father-in-law's money. Sir Harry refused to part with it. His son-in-law killed him. The key to the prosecution's case was a fingerprint of de Marigny's found on a

The accused Alfred de Marigny and his wife Nancy after the verdict. (UPI photo)

Chinese screen in Oakes's home. This was a crucial bit of evidence because de Marigny had already stated that he had not been in Westbourne for a long time.

The prosecutor brought in a long string of witnesses to establish various points in his case, e.g., the plaintiff's bad character, and then brought in his fingerprint expert, Captain Barker, who made a definite identification of the de Marigny print. When defense counsel Godfrey Higgs had finished with the expert, however, his identification was a little less certain. Through careful questioning, Higgs made several points which were highly damaging to Barker's testimony:

1. During cross-examination, Barker was no longer able to tell, as he had earlier asserted he could, which part of the screen the print had come from.

2. It is almost impossible to lift a print from a screen without lifting background along with it, yet the print that Barker had taken was perfectly clean, suspiciously clean.

3. Although it was standard practice to photograph a print where it had been found, Barker had failed to do so.

4. De Marigny had been taken into the murder room on the first day and had, with Barker's knowledge, been given several things to handle.

Higgs then partially demolished Christie's testimony by forcing him to admit that he had moved the body. He finished his defense by bringing in several witnesses who challenged many of the statements made by those who had testified for the state. The jury deliberated less than two and a half hours before finding de Marigny not guilty.

With that the case was effectively dropped. The duke and duchess had conveniently absented themselves from the Bahamas during the trial. As soon as possible they absented themselves permanently. No real attempt to solve the case was ever made. No one will ever know for sure who killed Sir Harry Oakes.

One theory about the murder that has been advanced in recent years is based on information received from two underworld informers. According to this theory the events that led to Harry's death were set in motion by his intransigence on the casino deal. The information from the informants and common sense suggest the following scenario:

Meyer Lansky was extremely upset with Sir Harry's change of

Meyer Lansky in 1951. Was he involved? (UPI photo)

mind and began to put strong pressure on Christie to mend matters. Christie knew what the underworld did to people who "crossed" them and realizing that Sir Harry was in danger, he attempted to change his mind. But Harry lived in his own intransigent world and told Christie that he would take no nonsense from these hoodlums.

When several blunt threats from Lansky signaled imminent violence, Christie stepped in as a peacemaker. Lansky agreed to send a lieutenant to talk, and the man arrived along with four button men in a fast power cruiser on the afternoon of July 7.

Late that evening Christie drove Sir Harry down to the docks and the two men went aboard the yacht. The conversation was short and to the point. Sir Harry quickly made it known that he had no intention of changing his mind and began to curse at the lieutenant, who then nodded slightly to one of his men. Bahama's number-one citizen went down like a felled tree as he was hit in the head by a four-pronged winch handle.

The lieutenant assured the now terrified Christie that Sir Harry was not dead, but had only been knocked out as a warning. One of the button men was assigned to help Christie get the inert Sir Harry back to Westbourne, but by the time they arrived there, it was obvious that he was not just unconscious—he was dead. Christie was paralyzed with fear. Lansky's man had the corpse undressed and put into pajamas. The bed was then burned, followed by the body. The feathers were a last-minute inspiration. With that the button man left Christie to his own devices and to the consequences of the tragic drama that was to follow.

This is a scenario that fits all the missing points. It explains Christie's frantic behavior and the bungling by Captain Barker. Still it is only a theory. The truth may never be known. There is an epilogue to this mystery. In 1963, exactly twenty years after Sir Harry's murder, sources indicate Meyer Lansky obtained his gambling monopoly in the Bahamas. The reported price was a little over one million dollars.

A Union Affair

ONE OF THE MOST mysterious and startling unsolved crimes of the century involved the disappearance of one of the most powerful and notorious men in America, a man who once controlled billions of dollars and who possessed economic clout capable of crippling the country and of influencing presidential elections.

Even in recent years, first while in jail and then while under parole restrictions, this man still had power sufficient to control hundreds of thousands and possibly millions of dollars and to move in the company of very influential and dangerous people. Toward the end of his life, his personal charisma was enough to make his resumption of absolute leadership in his union a strong possibility. It was a possibility that shook a lot of people and quite possibly sealed his death warrant. That man was Jimmy Hoffa.

The last day of Hoffa's life, Wednesday, July 30, 1975, began much like any other day. He breakfasted with his family at their modest summer home just north of Detroit. About 1 P.M. after puttering around the house during the morning, the former union boss left for a meeting in nearby Bloomfield Township. He was casual about the meeting, only telling his wife the name of the place he was going, a fashionable restaurant called the Machus Red Fox.

On his way to the restaurant, Jimmy stopped at the premises of a small business he had an interest in and spoke to employees there. During this conversation he named the men he planned to meet. The names told a lot about Jimmy Hoffa.

Among them was Detroit Mafia boss Anthony "Tony Jack" Giacalone. The other two were racketeer and former teamster official

Jimmy Hoffa on the way to prison in 1967.   (UPI photo)

Anthony "Tony Pro" Provenzano and Detroit labor leader Leonard Schultz.

Someone showed up, but no one knows who. Hoffa was seen standing in the restaurant parking lot, apparently waiting for someone. At 2:30 he called his wife to tell her that the people he expected had not come. That phone call was the last time anyone heard Jimmy Hoffa's voice.

Hoffa's family became deeply disturbed when he did not return home by that evening. After calling friends and a few union officials, the family spent the night waiting for developments. When morning came without a sign of Hoffa, the police were notified. A quick search of the restaurant parking lot turned up his car but not much else.

Although initial police efforts were fruitless, the police had an abundance of leads. Hoffa had a lot of enemies and his recent activities pointed to several people as possible suspects.

During the summer of 1975 Hoffa had been a man on the move. Paroled from prison in 1971 by President Nixon, he had been restive under the legal restrictions that went with his freedom. Chief among these was a ban on union activity.

Hoffa had led a very comfortable life after his release. He had a loving family and his assets, acquired in days of power, probably ran to over a million dollars. He owned a very comfortable home along with many of the amenities that most Americans consider to be the height of luxurious living.

But Jimmy was a very ambitious man. The struggle for power had consumed the better part of his life. It was his tough tactics that had, in effect, made the Teamsters the really potent union it had become. And it was also Jimmy Hoffa who had created those close ties between the union and the Mafia that had resulted in so much money for so many. He wanted power again, power and the chance to undo the people he considered his betrayers.

Jimmy appeared to be laying low for a long while after his release, but insiders knew he was quietly consolidating his position. In 1975 he felt a change in the climate of the country and the union. He sensed an opportunity to move back to center stage . . . and he took it.

Hoffa's chief rival was Teamsters President Frank Fitzsimmons. Fitzsimmons had been Hoffa's hand-picked successor, but during

Jimmy's time in jail and his early years on parole, Fitzsimmons solidified his control of the union and became his own man. Hoffa was clearly "out."

It was believed by many (including Hoffa) that Fitzsimmons was responsible for having the ban on union activity made a condition of Hoffa's parole. At the time of Hoffa's release, Richard Nixon was looking for some form of union support. The rank-and-file truckers wanted Hoffa out of jail. Fitzsimmons wanted to secure his position against any threat by Hoffa. Under the parole agreement worked out in 1971 everyone got what they wanted . . . except Jimmy.

The Teamsters held an election in 1976. If Hoffa was to make a move, the upcoming vote was his chance to do it. Jimmy was legally barred from taking office as Teamsters president, and his union activities would leave him in clear violation of his parole even if he didn't. But he calculated that a harried Gerald Ford, seeking election himself, would never move against the union that was his only base of labor support. Jimmy's main strength lay with the rank and file, who still remembered him as the man who built their union, and with a long list of union officials who owed their positions to Hoffa and who, in many cases, now feared that they would be replaced by Fitzsimmons' men.

Fitzsimmons' strength, on the other hand, lay with the many high Teamsters officials who appreciated his loose style of leadership, one which allowed the locals pretty much to have it their own way. Hoffa had run the union with a tight hand and many of these tough local leaders were very unhappy at the thought of giving up any of their new power.

The Mafia also was generally considered to be in Fitzsimmons' camp. It was Hoffa, of course, who had established ties between the underworld and the Teamsters but Fitzsimmons was the one who had really made the connection on a large scale. During Fitz's reign, money-making opportunities had, to an unprecedented degree, been offered to mobsters. The biggest single factor in Fitzsimmons' favor was Mafia use of the Teamster's infamous Central States, Southeast, and Southwest Areas Pension Fund. Some $1.3 billion are controlled by this fund (out of total pension funds of nearly $4 billion). Despite the big outlays for the pensions themselves and other expenses as well, the sum is so large that corrupt officials have

Chuckie O'Brien under pressure. He had nothing to say.   (UPI photo)

been able to siphon off millions upon millions of dollars into "loans" to the Mob.

Once Fitzsimmons opened the taps, the underworld used the fund (and other funds as well) to finance all sorts of typical Mob enterprises. The list includes hotels, casinos, country clubs, cemeteries, etc. Some examples are noteworthy. In the late 1960s, the fund lent the Boca Teeca Country Club $5.1 million. The club defaulted on the loan, but not before a key figure in the deal made a lot of money. North of San Diego some $100 million was spent to create a lavish spa called Rancho La Costa. The place is used as a fashionable watering hole by top Teamsters officials, underworld dons, and entertainment figures such as Bob Hope and Frank Sinatra. Teamsters pension funds contributed an estimated $57 million to the project. In Nevada, officials estimate that some $156 million in pension funds have been invested in gambling interests there since 1970. Obviously, this adds up to a great deal of money and the "Organization" could not have been happy over the prospect of anyone upsetting this extremely lucrative applecart. There existed then, in various quarters, plenty of motivation to have Hoffa eliminated.

Still more tension was added to the situation when rumors began to circulate that the former Teamster boss would testify about union Mafia ties as part of his reelection campaign. The result would be that indictments would be brought against Fitzsimmons. It is highly unlikely that Hoffa would have talked, but in the uncertain atmosphere of 1975 he actually might have been believable to some people.

The police investigation of the disappearance was difficult from the beginning. At first the federal authorities stayed out of the case, at least publicly. As a result the early work fell almost entirely on the five-man Bloomfield Township detective squad. Expertise on the squad was limited. So was their power. Commenting on his failure to question Mafia chieftain Giacalone, one Bloomfield policeman was quoted as saying, "You just don't go up and talk to someone like this."

Less than two weeks later the FBI officially entered the case (by then it was revealed that a federal-state crime task force had been watching the case from the beginning). The FBI took a much tougher and more professional approach to the crime, but in the end they

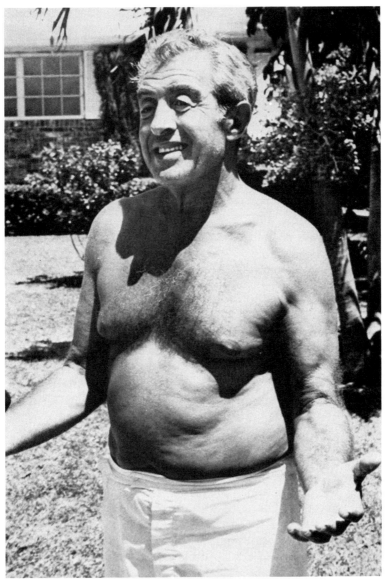

Anthony "Tony Pro" Provenzano—"Jimmy was . . . or is . . . my friend."
(UPI photo)

came up with little more information than had the Bloomfield detective squad.

Giacalone, Provenzano, and Schultz all denied having set up a meeting with Hoffa. Each of them made innocent-sounding statements and only Provenzano slipped up slightly when he said, "Jimmy was . . . or is . . . my friend." Despite the fact that all three had possible motives for doing Hoffa in, nothing concrete could be established against any of them.

Material clues were virtually nonexistent. There was nothing suspicious about the car Hoffa had left in the parking lot. Nothing else was found. A few witnesses were found who verified his presence in the restaurant lot and this supported his statement that he intended to meet the three men, but there was not enough to add up to anything definite.

As national publicity came to the case, a variety of anonymous tips poured in. Jimmy Hoffa was on board a yacht on Lake Michigan; his body was buried in a cornfield; he was hiding out in Upper Michigan. All the tips were checked, but none of them amounted to anything.

The only lead that looked promising was the one that led to Hoffa's adopted son, Charles "Chuckie" O'Brien. Chuckie had been adopted by the Hoffas when he was three years old. Raised with Hoffa's son and daughter, he had been part of the family until he grew older. Heavyset, with a beer belly, he had become known as a liar and a financially irresponsible person. He was a striking contrast to Hoffa's other son James Jr., who was the image of trim respectability.

Chuckie had eventually become a $45,000-a-year union organizer (and had been one of the men responsible for the Teamsters' campaign against Cesar Chavez and the United Farm Workers). During the few years prior to his father's death he had grown further and further apart from him and closer and closer to Fitzsimmons, who had rewarded Chuckie's change of sides by promoting him within the union hierarchy, and Giacalone, who had been close to him all his life (he called the mob boss "Uncle Tony" or "Uncle Jack").

The day after his father disappeared, Chuckie also dropped out of sight. He turned up five days later and was immediately questioned by the FBI whereupon he told a confused story that had him driving in the vicinity of the Machus Red Fox near the time of the abduction in a car borrowed from Giacalone's son. Although they couldn't pin anything definite on him, the FBI remained highly suspicious of Chuckie. Among other things the agents reasoned that even at gunpoint the tough Hoffa would never get into a car with a stranger.

Reports leaked out to the press that agents had seized the borrowed car and that bloodstains had been found in the back seat. The rift between Chuckie and his family came out in the open and he quickly became unwelcome at the Hoffa house.

Thousands of man-hours of investigation were poured into the case but one by one all the leads seemed to come to nothing. Suspicions and bits of evidence abounded, but in true gangster fashion, substantial clues were absent. In the end, the authorities were left to speculate on what really happened. Several possibilities arose.

Some felt that Hoffa was murdered by someone within the union who feared Hoffa would succeed in unseating Fitzsimmons. A top aide or even an outsider associated with the union might have taken it upon himself to "stablize" things.

Others close to the case believed that the Mob murdered Jimmy. Hoffa knew a lot about Mafia business and its tremendous involvement in union activities and funds. He had already threatened to talk as part of his election campaign. As mentioned before, most people doubted that Jimmy would really break silence, but in recent years he had come to be known as unreliable. Big Mob bosses with a lot to lose might well have decided to nip possible trouble in the bud. It had been done before for stakes which were a lot smaller.

A third possibility involved Jimmy's outside dealings. He was into countless money ventures. One of them may have backfired. A fourth had Hoffa disappearing for his own reasons, but this theory died quickly.

Generally speaking, however, authorities still feel that one or more of those individuals named in this chapter was the hand behind the death. Investigators pursued this line heavily and for a while it looked like they might have something. In December of 1975 federal sources reported that an informer had accused Tony Provenzano of masterminding the crime. Three "Tony Pro" associates in New Jersey were fingered as the hit men. According to the story Hoffa's body was stuffed into a fifty-five-gallon oil drum, carted to New Jersey, and buried in a swamp. For a few weeks it looked as though the case might be solved. But then, as so often happens in Mafia-related cases, the story broke down. No body was found in the swamp and the necessary testimony was not forthcoming. The Feds turned back to their investigative work.

In the years since then, a veritable mountain of information has been dug through and countless people have been interviewed, but the FBI is no closer to solving the mystery now than it was at the beginning. The case is still open, but for all practical purposes the enigmatic story of what happened to Jimmy Hoffa, and who did it, will puzzle the public for years to come.

Death on the Cross Bell

IN 1970 THE CROSS BELL RANCH in Oklahoma was one of the largest in the world. Nobody, even the owner, seemed quite sure how big it really was. Most people guessed in excess of 100,000 acres, but no one knew. It stretched across the vast Oklahoma plains farther than the eye could see. Inside its boundaries, hundreds of men worked, their material needs met by a small city of their own. Huge herds of cattle roamed to the far corners of the holdings and only planes and motor vehicles could keep up with them.

The owners lived in a style that was pure Hollywood. Young E. C. Mullendore chartered private planes when he wanted to travel, and that was often. New Cadillacs graced his compound every year. When he decided to join a country club in nearby Bartlesville he spent over $200,000 on a house in town so that he could avoid commuting. When he entertained, the caterers came from Texas.

E. C.'s wife, Linda, was no slouch at spending either. Dressing in the finest clothes, she did most of her shopping at Neiman-Marcus in Houston (she would fly in on shopping sprees). During one two-year period she and her sister ran up $100,000 in bills.

Throughout Oklahoma and as far away as Texas and California the Mullendores and the Cross Bell were known as the epitome of Western wealth and flash. They had everything, it seemed, that any American family could dream of.

Then, on the night of September 26, 1970, E. C. was found in the basement of his house with a bullet hole in his forehead. Blood dripping from his body, he was carried by shocked ranch hands to the nearest hospital. A few hours later the handsome ranching heir was dead.

As news of the bizarre circumstances surrounding the shooting began to leak out (despite efforts to suppress it), the first hints of scandal reached the newspapers. All was not what it seemed on the Cross Bell and with the violent death of E. C., a story began to unfold that would intrigue a nation and reveal a web of financial finagling that would touch some of America's biggest corporations and run into the millions of dollars. It was a tale that would include some of the underworld's seamiest characters as well as some of the financial world's most irreproachable men. Deeply tangled in it are greed, illusions, and the Western Dream. It may serve for many as a parable of modern America.

The story begins with Gene Mullendore, the family patriarch and the founding force behind the Cross Bell. Gene was a crusty man, hard and penny-pinching in business. From his earliest days he had been brought up to respect the value of land and to dream of owning unlimited quantities of it. Starting with his family's assets, he took advantage of the Depression and a series of powerful friendships to form a ranching empire.

In 1959, E. C. left his fourth year of college to return to the Cross Bell and take over from his dad. In the same year he also married his childhood sweetheart, Linda Vance. They were installed in a new house Gene built for them across the swimming pool, opposite the main mansion.

From the beginning, E. C. had big ideas for the Cross Bell. A product of the postwar period, he wanted to modernize the ranch and turn it into a huge agricultural machine. At first, because Gene remained in control behind the scenes, progress was slow. But over the years E. C. became the real boss and began to put his imprint on the land. What he created was a little different from what he had intended.

What undid E. C. was his total lack of discipline in money matters. Raised in an environment where everything was flown in from stores in Houston and Dallas, E. C. had no understanding of limited assets or what happens when you use up what you have. Running out of money was not on his list of experiences.

E. C. Mullendore before his problems.   (UPI photo)

Soon gone were the convict ranch hands that Gene had used so effectively as cheap labor. Wages rose and alongside came fringe benefits that included everything from free groceries to free medical care. E. C. was a soft touch and the Cross Bell soon gained a wide reputation as a great place to work.

At the same time E. C. began to sink ever-increasing amounts of money into long-range schemes to upgrade the ranch. Hundreds of thousands were spent on stud bulls and prize cattle. Swamp lands were cleared and heavy equipment purchased to level it. Plans for all these endeavors were laid over coffee or during late night bull sessions with friends. E. C. had no formal training in management (Gene had sent him off to study banking). He knew the course of day-to-day ranch operations from his childhood but seldom had he any real grasp of what the long-range consequences of his actions might be. When he saw something he wanted to do, he did it. When he needed a little money, he went down to a local bank and asked for it. The Mullendore credit was *very* good.

By 1969, E. C. owed a variety of financial institutions some $8 million. The land value of the ranch was well over twice that much, but the interest payments were exceeding ranch income and it was obvious that things could not continue as they were for much longer. The situation was further aggravated by the Mullendores' refusal to accept any limitations on their life-style. Despite their growing indebtedness, the shopping trips to Neiman-Marcus continued unabated. New Cadillacs continued to adorn the mansion compound and old Gene continued to have expensive, unremunerative playthings (which included maintaining nonprofit herds of longhorn cattle, buffalo, and a walk-in birdhouse that cost more than twenty thousand dollars).

Using the only tactic he understood, E. C. decided to look for one big umbrella loan to consolidate all the smaller ones. Finding he was unable to walk into the average bank or life-insurance company and get an $8 million "bill-payer" loan, E. C. turned to his hustler brother-in-law, who recommended two "super insurance salesmen" in Atlanta, Leroy Kerwin and Leon Cohen.

Kerwin and Cohen are a story unto themselves. Kerwin (under another name), got his start in the early 1960s in Chicago, where he opened a Ford dealership on borrowed money, sold three hundred

74

cut-rate cars to the Mafia in two days, and then declared bankruptcy. Cohen was a convicted rapist and stock swindler. Joining forces in 1969, the two set up a new racket in life insurance as they tried to stay one step ahead of the IRS. The racket took its impetus from the greed shown by new life-insurance companies.

To get them started, insurance companies commonly pay new agents a 55 percent commission of the first year's sales. Styling himself a supersalesman, Cohen talked new companies into giving him 90 percent or more. Within a very short time, the two con men sold more than $40 million worth of insurance. Unfortunately for the companies, most of the policy owners failed to renew after the first year.

They failed to renew because Kerwin and Cohen were really in the business of selling loans. With a huge life-insurance policy to show, panicky borrowers had more leverage with banks or other lending organizations, or could, if necessary, turn to the Mafia (the Mafia often required a life-insurance policy as big as the loan in order to make sure that, one way or the other, the borrower paid up). Kerwin and Cohen pocketed both the insurance commission and that part of the loan given them as a finder's fee. By moving rapidly from company to company, their reputation for amounts sold traveled faster than the cancellations that followed them. And it was all legal, just barely.

Kerwin and Cohen put on a big show for E. C., spending money like there was no tomorrow in restaurants and on chauffeured limousines. It was the kind of behavior E. C. understood (he wasn't known for looking too deeply into things) and he promptly agreed to take out $10 million in life insurance on himself and $5 million on Linda.

The new insurance company was overjoyed at the policy. As part of its background check, an investigator from the Retail Credit Company was sent to the Cross Bell to appraise the Mullendore assets. Apparently he had never handled anything this big before because after a lot of sweet talk from E. C. and Gene and an endless ride over the property, he turned in a net-worth estimate of $37,427,500, a wildly exaggerated figure that would be used again and again in future dealings.

Once the policy was issued, Kerwin and Cohen assured E. C. that the loan wouldn't be far behind. But while he was waiting he was forced to deal with the ever-increasing demands of his creditors. Although he was sometimes rather naive financially, E. C. had worked out a temporary system for dealing with bills that, had they thought of it, would have made the insurance agents proud. First, because of his image and the size of the Cross Bell, he was still able to get loans from small banks. Those in Oklahoma were wary, but that didn't stop E. C. Chartering a jet he would fly over to Georgia or to some other state where he had some sort of introduction and there bluff his way into a few thousand. His new credit rating, established by the insurance policy, made this even easier than before.

When this sort of finagling didn't work, E. C. would "kite checks." A bank would welcome his new account, made with a deposit of, say, $100,000. The only catch was that checks totaling $100,000 written by E. C. were already in the bank waiting to be processed. These checks would be coming from another bank where E. C. had an account and would be covering still other checks at another bank. Between this, the clever use of weekends (because banks are closed then), and the willingness of some bankers to sit on a check for a few days for a "good old boy," E. C. was able to squeeze through the difficult periods.

Amazingly, the large number of banks, life-insurance companies, and credit unions with which he dealt, never taxed E. C. with these fraudulent practices. Unlike the average working man who may be harassed if he bounces a check or misses a few payments, E. C. was never required to do more than have a friendly chat or give a few worthless assurances. Money institutions, it seems, have two sets of standards. In this case, they lived to regret it.

It soon became obvious that Kerwin and Cohen weren't coming up with the loan. They managed to sweet-talk E. C. into purchasing another $5 million worth of life insurance but he turned elsewhere for a "loan arranger." Word of the Cross Bell's plight—and its owner's gullibility—began to spread through the underworld. Stranger and stranger figures began to show up with promises of securing the big loan.

E. C. turned virtually no one away. Some he even put on his

payroll. Almost all of these shady people had prison records. The most sinister of all, Kent Green, took up residence on the Cross Bell along with his "wife." Both of them carried automatics and quickly intimidated the rest of the Mullendores. Green claimed access to Mafia money and even introduced E. C. to some well-known hoods.

During this period, E. C.'s life went steadily downhill. He became an alcoholic and was constantly drunk. Chub Anderson, the ranch foreman and himself an ex-con, was assigned to guard him constantly. It wasn't an easy task. E. C. flew all over the country at the drop of a hat, sometimes looking for a loan or sometimes just out of drunkenness. His life had also been threatened more than once by some of the thugs who surrounded him.

Finally, this house of cards began to fall apart. Linda moved out and prior to divorce filed for separate maintenance. Because the lending institutions were threatening to force sale of land to get their money back, Gene tried to get E. C. to declare himself bankrupt as a way of keeping the ranch intact. One of the principal creditors dug its heels in and demanded payment immediately. All this occurred during September, 1970. By September 26, E. C. was dead.

The murder investigation was botched from the beginning. The ranch was in the country and straddled two counties. Neither county sheriff cooperated with the other and neither was competent in homicide investigation. What few clues were at the scene were either misinterpreted or destroyed. Quick work by the embalmer did the rest.

Chub, the foreman, was the only witness. He claimed after E. C. was shot, he entered the room where the crime was committed and found two men there, whom he chased away. Chub had bad head wounds and a bullet hole in his shoulder to support his story. He said he didn't get a good look at the assailants.

Some people talked about suicide. E. C. had been shot in the head point blank, but no paraffin test was ordered on E. C.'s hand until after he was washed at the mortuary.

The local authorities were embarrassed. E. C. was a powerful figure and they were clearly unable fo find those responsible for his death. They dropped the case as quickly as possible. There matters would have lain except for the insurance policies. E. C. had conveniently died just a few days before his $10 million life-insurance policy was due to lapse. Needless to say, the insurance companies were more than a little reluctant to pay up.

As is customary with policies that big, the liability for it had been spread around (along with another $5 million policy E. C. picked up later) among several major companies. These companies quickly formed a high-powered group of lawyers and executives to handle the case and after a few conferences they set out to prove that E. C. had committed suicide.

For several months hostility was rife in Oklahoma as the various parties fought it out in the courts and in the press. For a while it looked like the bitterness between Gene and Linda Mullendore might solve everything for the insurance companies. Gene and Linda had never liked each other. The only thing they had in common after E. C.'s death was their hurry to get their hands on the Cross Bell. But in the end, moved by the cold light of reality and aided by attorneys, they drew up a written agreement dividing up the spoils. The insurance companies pressed on but it soon became apparent that it would be very difficult to substantiate suicide. In December, 1971, the various lawyers got together out of court and the insurance companies agreed to pay $8 million.

The money was paid the following January. Linda got $3 million. The rest went to pay off as many of the family debts as possible. Immediately after the settlement Linda's lawyer divorced his wife. In June, he married Linda.

As per his agreement with his daughter-in-law, Gene was left with the ranch. He was forced into bankruptcy proceedings but managed to hold on to actual title until he died in 1973. One of his last acts was to order a monument built over E. C.'s grave. He had the bill sent to bankruptcy court.

Leroy Kerwin was killed in Canada in 1971, apparently because of money he owed the Mafia. Leon Cohen is still looking for a new way to make money.

Many people hoped that after the insurance settlement the mystery over E. C.'s death would be solved. A grand jury was convened and several witnesses heard, including Gene and Linda, but no action was ever taken. Reporters have nibbled at the case since, but amazingly no solid indication of who killed E. C. has ever been uncovered. There were no witnesses besides Chub. No murder weapon was found. There were no fingerprints or tire marks. Theories about the case abound, but hard facts pertaining to it are virtually nonexistent.

Did E. C. commit suicide to end his money problems once and for all? Did Chub kill him for similar reasons? Did a member of the family want the insurance money? Was the Mafia involved? It may be that no one will ever know. The investigations have ended. Those who could have spoken have begun new lives and lapsed into silence. The original Cross Bell is gone, swallowed up by modern agriculture and big corporations. New people work the ranch and walk on the land where E. C.'s death took place. Only the mystery lingers on, a violent enigma to tantalize crime buffs for decades to come.

MARRIAGE
AND DEATH

"Love and marriage, love and marriage,
Go together like a horse and carriage."

They also go with Death. Passion, jealousy, and bad marriages have helped to fill police files for centuries. For the suspicious wife, the vengeful father, or the outraged family, misplaced love is the classic incitement to crime.

A Tragedy in Texas

CONNIE HILL RAN EXCITEDLY up the long sidewalk to the front door of her Houston home. The cab that had brought her from the airport was still at the curb, her husband John inside. Connie was happy, as happy as she had ever been in her life. Her four-day honeymoon was over and it had seemed to underscore the new beginning of her life.

Ringing the bell of the stately home, she pressed her face against the glass, looking for a glimpse of her stepson. John's twelve-year-old child by a former marriage had grown very close to Connie and she knew he would be anxious to hear all about their trip.

At first there was no answer. Then as Connie peered down the hall a figure appeared and started for the door. At first Connie thought the figure was Robert dressed up in a Halloween costume. She smiled to herself. His constant playfulness towards her made her feel warm and secure in her new home.

As the figure moved to open the door, Connie suddenly realized that it was too tall to be Robert. Before she could think again the door opened and the figure in green reached out and dragged her into the house by the neck. Fear raced through Connie and she opened her mouth to scream. At the same time she saw the black pistol in the figure's hand. As the deadly weapon pointed towards her head she closed her mouth in silence.

"This is a robbery." A male voice spoke from behind the strange green mask. At the same time Connie's husband came up behind her. Suddenly he had his hands upon the intruder and she was free. As the two men grappled in the doorway, Connie began to run

85

frantically towards a neighbor's house. She didn't even make it out of the yard before she heard the first shot. Then a second. Then a third.

Within minutes, police cars filled the area, neighbors streamed out of nearby houses, and a terrified twelve-year-old boy and his grandmother had been led outside for first aid and comfort. Connie returned to find the body of her husband just inside the doorway. Tape covered his nose, mouth, and eyes. Blood soaked the tapes and also appeared on other parts of his body. John Hill, wealthy plastic surgeon and, as we shall see, a man accused of murdering his first wife, was dead. Vengeance, in a case that involved some of Texas' most wealthy and powerful people, had come full circle.

To understand the case and the double murders, adultery, and legal shenanigans that accompanied it we must go back to 1957 to become acquainted with the seemingly innocent beginnings that, somehow developed into one of the most bizarre murder cases of our times.

The cast of characters is as follows:

Ash Robinson—a heavyset, crusty, oil baron who made his money the hard way and stepped on anyone who got in his way as he did it. Used to power and big money, he was a man to be reckoned with in Texas politics. Although he had the wealth and influence to get what he wanted, little in life interested him as much as his beloved daughter, Joan.

Joan Robinson—Twenty-seven, the adored only child of a multimillionaire, an attractive blond who was over protected and spoiled from the time she was born. She traveled in the jet-set world of boom-time Texas, and her name was constantly bandied about in local society columns. Her only real love was horses. She started riding when she was four and by the time she was twenty-three, was one of the most famous horsewomen in America. Despite the fact that she did a lot of dating and had already gone through two marriages, her private life was often empty. Always just daddy's little girl, by 1957, Joan was becoming troubled by the meaninglessness of her life.

John Hill—a young plastic surgeon with big ambitions about big money. Reared in a small South Texas town by a stern, Bible-quoting mother, he was socially shy—a mama's boy, some

86

would say. His real love was music and he was already an accomplished performer on several instruments by the time he graduated from medical school in Houston. Music was the only thing that detracted from his zeal to make it in the Houston medical world.

John and Joan met by accident one night in 1957 at a fashionable restaurant in Houston. Something about the boyish-but-handsome young doctor intrigued Joan and she set her cap for him. It didn't take long.

To many close friends, the couple seemed totally incompatible. They had virtually nothing in common and their main interests, horses and music, were utterly disparate. But there was one way in which they did seem very well-matched. Twice divorced and approaching thirty, Joan longed for a permanent and respectable marriage partner. John, for his part, knew very well how important an attractive and prominent wife could be to an aspiring plastic surgeon.

The two were married in a huge, storybook wedding paid for by Ash Robinson. It was the kind of social event that people talk about for years. Shortly after the ceremony, the newlyweds moved into an upstairs room of the Robinson mansion and John got back to the business of his medical education, with all cost now paid by his father-in-law.

At first everything went smoothly. Joan really loved John and in the beginning he acted like he loved her. Although Joan's equestrian hobby kept her away from her husband for long periods of time, he was deeply involved in both his schooling and music and insisted that he didn't mind. Ash was very happy with the arrangement. He still had his darling daughter under his roof and could spend a lot of time with her.

Gradually, however, things began to change. Joan began to realize that her husband cared little for what she did. He fell asleep at her riding competitions, when he came at all.

At the same time he devoted almost all his spare time to his real passion, classical music. Drawing on his wife's unlimited resources (the contents of her father's pocket), John started work on his longtime dream, a private music room. John did not dream small. The project he embarked on would have enhanced a big-city opera house. One of the world's best custom-made pianos, hundreds of speakers, huge chandeliers, and vast spaces to ensure good acoustics were a few of the accoutrements that eventually ran the bill for his dream into the hundreds of thousands of dollars. Joan watched in angry silence, unable to deny him but unhappy over the growing alienation his obsession produced. No break was evident yet, but beneath the surface, it had begun.

Over the next few years, John's career flourished. He joined a private practice and despite dark signs that he was perhaps a bit unscrupulous and unreliable, his income rose steadily and his public image inproved. In 1960, the Hills had a son and, even though the father was less than enthusiastic about the event, it further enhanced his status. It also made Ash deliriously happy. Being a grandfather had been one of his fondest wishes and he promptly "adopted" the baby as his own.

For a long time, life for the Hills continued more or less normally, frequently strained, but with no real signs of a change. Then, one hot August day in 1968, John went to pick up his son at summer camp and the seeds for tragedy were sown.

John had not wanted to make the trip. He had progressively drawn further and further away from the roles of father and husband and had become increasingly more involved in making money and making music. Only a fierce tirade from Joan had forced him to play the father this time.

John hadn't been at the camp for very long before he saw someone that took his mind off his son and changed his life forever. That someone was divorcée Ann Kurth.

Three-times married and approaching forty, Ann Kurth still had the kind of soft voluptuous body that made men stare. She resembled Elizabeth Taylor and she liked to flaunt the resemblance. John Hill took one look at her and for the first time in his life, was sexually overwhelmed. For the rest of the day, he pursued his new interest all across the camp. A few days later, he stopped at her home to deliver some pictures he had taken. He left at dawn the next morning.

Within a very short time, John announced to Ann that she was to consider herself his woman. "What about you wife?" she asked. "That," John answered, "is over. It's just a matter of time."

By the end of the month John was hopelessly involved. Sexually

repressed all his life, he had finally found someone who could unleash the desire for physical pleasure in him. Even his wife, much to
her regret, had been unable to break through the walls raised by his
moralistic upbringing. Usually a careful and somewhat cynical man in
business, John threw caution to the winds and moved in openly with
Ann.

Joan was stunned, heartbroken, and furious. John had left only a
brief note, and then refused to speak to her on the telephone. For
days after the move she kept the secret to herself, telling only a few
friends. Then, one morning over coffee (every morning he was in
Houston, Ash came over to talk with his daughter), she broke down
and told her father. He was furious and wanted to take action immediately. He'd show that pipsqueak who was who. But Joan
wouldn't have it. She was still lost in love and she grabbed at any ray
of hope she could find. First she tried frantically to get in touch with
John. Then she decided to give him time. Then she searched his car.
Nothing made any difference and nothing changed. John continued
to live with Ann Kurth and he even began to flaunt his relationship
with her in public. Seemingly oblivious to gossip, he introduced her
to all of his acquaintances and, in the process, began to make himself
a social outcast. Finally, in mid-November, Joan was served with
divorce papers.

With that, Ash Robinson stepped in. Deferring to his daughter's
desperate pleas, the doughty old man had until now limited himself
to driving by the Kurth place and hiring a detective to follow his
son-in-law. Now, incensed at the hurt and shame his daughter felt,
he made a phone call to him. That was all it took.

No one knows what the millionaire said to the doctor during that
call or of what the subsequent hurried meeting at the Robinson
mansion consisted, but money and John's son must have been the
central topics. Ash apparently threatened to cut John off from
everything—the Robinson money, the music room, and any hopes
for a career in Houston.

Whatever was said, Ash obtained a signed statement from John
promising eternal love and devotion to Joan. The letter was highly
apologetic, and self-demeaning. It also contained a condition. Any
further dalliances by John would cost him everything he owned.

He moved back into his home but little had changed. Within days he was back in the arms of his mistress. Ann was a demanding woman. John couldn't have given her up even if he had wanted to, and it was perfectly clear that he didn't. At first, he acted surreptitiously. He began to be called away more for late night surgery. Emergency calls began to come with increasing frequency.

In the beginning, Joan didn't seem to notice. She was too happy to have her husband back. She planned big parties and worked frantically to make herself look as attractive as possible. But gradually the truth forced itself upon her.

On March 9, 1969, two women arrived at the Hill house as Joan's guests. That evening the guests and the Hills dined out. In the middle of the meal, John was called away by a telephone page. To Joan's anger, he did not return until after eleven that night. When he did come back he was ebullient. He had brought pastries with him and, refusing the help of the ladies, served them himself, insisting that each woman eat what was served her. On March 11, a Tuesday night, the same scene was repeated, an interrupted dinner, a prolonged absence, and then John's determined serving of pastries.

Hostility mounted as the week passed. John stayed away longer and longer and his excuses were flimsier and flimsier. Joan's anger slowly simmered in front of her house guests. Then, on Friday night, John snubbed her in front of some of Houston's most prominent people. She boiled over. In a screaming late-night confrontation she poured out all of her hate, hurt, and frustration. John stormed into his car and drove away. Joan cursed him and made up her mind that the marriage was over. It was, but not in the way she expected.

Joan did not wake up until four the next afternoon. She was surprised at how much she had slept and felt a little off-color, but made it through what was left of the day. The next morning when she woke up there was no doubt that she was ill. Pale and shaking she made her way downstairs to greet her guests only to find on getting there that she had to throw up.

John tucked his wife into bed, dismissing any notion that the illness might be serious. "Probably something she ate," he told the guests. Leaving them to tend to his wife, John went out. As usual he did not return until late.

The guests were due to leave the following morning. It was Monday. Joan was no better, still vomiting whenever she tried to eat, but

90

Dr. Hill insisted that it was only a minor stomach ailment and shooed Joan's friends on their way. When the maid arrived, John ordered her to let Joan have complete rest. She should not see or speak to anyone, even on the telephone.

The maid spent the day taking phone calls from Joan's concerned friends and acquaintances, insisting that Joan was unable to speak with them. Finally, when nothing had been heard from Joan's room, the maid, contrary to Dr. Hill's explicit instructions, looked in. She found her ashen-faced employer awake and very feeble. "I'm so sick," was all Joan could manage to say. The maid comforted her and returned to the kitchen to wait worriedly for Dr. Hill to come home.

Joan's condition deteriorated rapidly. The next morning, the maid, instructed by John to clean up her mistress, found Joan lying in a mess of blood and excrement. Dried feces indicated that Joan had not been tended to at all during the night. As the maid worked to wash away the stains, she noticed that Joan had a raging fever. "I don't want to die," Joan gasped in a moment of lucidity. The maid comforted her. "You're not going to die," she said. But when she finished cleaning, she got down on her knees and prayed.

Now things began to happen quickly. Summoned by the maid, John returned around lunchtime. It hadn't been easy to get away. He had had to break a date with Ann Kurth, and she had been very unhappy about it. John was joined quickly by Ash Robinson and his wife. John promptly announced that he was taking Joan to the hospital—not the famed Texas Medical Center which was only 15 minutes away, but a small suburban hospital where he insisted she would get special care. In front of an astonished Ash who until now had no idea there was anything seriously wrong with his daughter), John forced his wife to walk to their car, and with Joan and Ash's wife, drove away.

When they pulled up to the small hospital, they found that it didn't even have an emergency room, and that apparently no one had been alerted to Joan's impending arrival. Joan was taken to a private room and was put through the normal hospital admitting procedures. Her blood pressure was found to be so low that the possibility of death had to be taken into account. The doctor assigned to the case was summoned immediately.

Dr. Bertinot was only slightly acquainted with the Hills. A capable, though hardly reknowned young physician, he had been surprised when John had telephoned and asked him to look after his wife, who was apparently suffering from stomach flu. He was even more surprised when the nurse called to inform him that Joan's life was in danger.

Dr. Bertinot rushed to Joan's bedside, and immediately ordered emergency procedures. Large amounts of intravenous fluids were pumped into her to try to raise her blood pressure. Sensing that she was suffering from some sort of massive general infection, Bertinot ordered what tests he could, but with the hospital's limited facilities there was little that could be done.

By late afternoon Joan's kidneys failed completely. The kidney specialist who was now called in vetoed a suggestion to move her to a larger hospital that had a kidney machine, because it was unsafe to move someone in her critical condition. The staff jury-rigged a device to help the kidney. Before the procedure could be started the hospital needed Dr. Hill's permission. But John had disappeared. Frantic calls were made. At 9:15 p.m. the good doctor was located at home, playing music. An hour and forty-five minutes later, he finally appeared at the hospital.

By 1:30 p.m. everything that could be done had been done. Leaving the patient in the care of night nurses, the attending doctors went home. John retired to a hall sofa to sleep.

Around 2:30 p.m., Joan went into sudden heart failure. The duty nurse ran for help, but it was too late. Joan sat up abruptly in her bed and cried out her husband's name. Then blood shot out of her mouth and she fell back, motionless. She was dead.

In the morning, the odd events continued. When the doctors arrived to do the autopsy they found the body had been sent on to the funeral home "by accident." When they got to the funeral home they found the body had already been drained of fluids and was partially embalmed, making any thorough autopsy difficult.

John didn't seem particularly upset by Joan's death. Other than making funeral arrangements and contacting the necessary people, he did little to alter his normal schedule. Ann Kurth was shocked at first, but she recovered very quickly. It didn't take her long to size up her new situation. Ash Robinson was in shock for a long time. His dearest possession had been taken from him, and in a manner so swift as to be incomprehensible. For two days the old man did little but try to get the facts straight in his mind. He talked quietly with friends and thought and thought and thought. The conclusions he came to were grim.

The morning of his daughter's funeral Ash presented himself to the district attorney and asked that a charge of murder be lodged against his son-in-law. The D.A. was taken aback by the demand, but Ash Robinson was not a man to be trifled with. Neither was the high-powered lawyer that accompanied him. The D.A. said he would think about it.

But Ash wanted more than thinking. A man who was used to getting his way, he began a one-man campaign to put John Hill on trial. He consulted with some of the best doctors in Houston and began having informal talks with them at his mansion. Tirelessly, he ran down every lead he could find. He hired a private detective to follow John. And he pestered the D.A.'s office continually, calling, stopping in, and sending friends to intercede for him.

It is highly unlikely that the circumstances of Joan's death would ever had been questioned if her father had been anyone else besides Ash Robinson. It is also possible that the whole matter would have been laid to rest if John had been a little more in control of himself where his attachment to Ann Kurth was concerned.

In the first months after Joan's death, John seemed to enjoy his new freedom. Ann became his constant companion. At first he practiced a certain amount of discretion, but he soon began to see her openly. They frequented the best clubs and restaurants and made no secret of their feeling for each other. Less than three months after Joan's death, over the bitter protests of his lawyer, John Hill married Ann in a civil ceremony. Suddenly, even the D.A. began listening to Ash's constant harping. Here, at last was a motive for murder. The stage was set for the next act in the tragedy.

The district attorney had struggled for some time with the problem that Joan's death had caused him. The D.A.'s office is a political one and Ash Robinson had a lot of clout. At the same time, it would have been almost impossible to get even an indictment on a charge which had virtually no substantive evidence in back of it. In the beginning the D.A. had dismissed the old man's accusations as grief-stricken ramblings. But the longer he listened, the more the D. A. sensed that there was something very strange about the way that Joan had died. By now Ash and his friends had come up with several theories: John had put some form of poison or bacterial infection in the pastries he served; John had injected Joan with some virulent form of infection. It was known that he had given his late wife several shots, but what was in the syringes was not known; John had given Joan tainted medicine.

Under pressure from Ash a grand jury was impaneled, but they failed to indict. A second grand jury was convened, but still no indictment was delivered.

Then John did it again. Towards the end of the year, after less than eight months of marriage, John went to court to divorce Ann Kurth. His lawyer threw up his hands. It was dangerous to make an enemy of Ann and by so doing John was playing into Ash's hands. The lawyer pleaded with him, but he was adamant. Life had turned miserable with Ann and he wanted out. In John's eyes she had proven to be a vicious, possessive, and highly jealous woman.

Immediately following the divorce proceedings, she hurried to the D. A.'s office. She had some stories to tell.

When the third grand jury met, Ash pulled out all the stops. He had a close personal friend installed as jury foreman. He lined up an impressive array of doctors to testify. To cap the medical testimony, he hired the foremost legal pathologist in the country (the New York City Medical Examiner) to reexamine the body and testify.

Ash spared no expense. Utilizing local laws, he financed the grand jury and virtually ran the hearing. For the *pièce de résistance* he produced Ann Kurth, who testified that not only had John confessed to killing Joan, he had, on more than one occasion tried to kill her as well.

To help the proceedings the D. A. came up with a more easily proven charge. Burrowing deep into obscure case histories, he discovered the crime of murder by neglect. He then charged that John Hill had willfully denied his wife adequate medical care and in so doing caused her death. It was unusual, to some even objectionable, but it got him an indictment.

The trial started in March of 1971, just a few days short of the second anniversary of Joan's death. Despite everything, John's lawyer was optimistic about its outcome. He felt that the state had no solid proof, nothing that would hold up in open court.

John Hill was optimistic, too. Not only did he believe in his lawyer, but he had found a new woman, Connie Loesby, and she seemed to be a combination of everything that John's first two wives had lacked. She was beautiful in a quiet, gentle way, she loved classical music (they had met at a concert) and she wanted to be supportive of John in all he did. They wanted to marry before the trial, but this time John listened to his lawyer—Connie stayed quietly in the background. So they could be together, she gave music lessons to John's son, a ruse which allowed the lovers a few quiet moments in the music room after her teaching was done.

Most of the trial went much as expected. Both sides had lined up impressive groups of witnesses and their testimony went on for days. The prosecution's star witness, was, of course, Ann Kurth. It is generally against the law for a wife to testify against her husband. It was difficult for the prosecution to get Ann on the stand, and the judge only allowed it when he heard what direction her testimony would take. The defense objected strenuously and demanded a mistrial, but to no avail. The judge was inclined to hear Ann's testimony. The prosecution knew what she said would be shocking but it would prove a lot more shocking than they realized.

It was obvious to everyone that Ann relished her time in the limelight. Despite the prosecution's counseling against it, she chose to appear in a seductive outfit. Her manner was emotional and she brought every ounce of melodrama that she could to her well-rehearsed story.

On the first day she testified about John's character and damned him on every side. He was cruel to her and had been cruel to his first wife. He was a poor father, a poor husband, and, by inference, a poor lover. The defense objected over and over again. Not only was a wife an illegal witness, her testimony was straying further and further from the prosecution's expressly stated desire to bring out testimony relating only to the time before she married John.

Then, in the middle of a rehearsed statement to the prosecutor, Ann, perhaps exhilarated by her position, began to say too much. She suddenly blurted out that John had told her about killing Joan. The prosecutor was stunned. He had carefully gone over what constituted inadmissible testimony with Ann and this was part of it. The defense was on its feet demanding a mistrial. Less than two hours later the judge granted it.

John and Connie were jubilant. The defense lawyer had assured them that it was most unlikely that a new trial would be ordered after what had happened. John was unhappy that he had been denied the opportunity to win acquittal and clear his reputation, but he looked forward to a new life with Connie.

Ash was stunned. He knew as well as the defense lawyer that a new trial would be hard to get. He was an old and bitter man. Hate raged inside him—hate and ironclad determination to see the matter through to the end.

A respectable amount of time after the trial, John and Connie were married. It was obvious from the beginning that John had finally found a woman he could be happy with. Life was difficult at first. John's practice had disintegrated during the scandal. There wasn't much money left, but they managed. They were not received well in Houston but as time passed they were gradually accepted. John was obviously happy with Connie, and the terrible events of the past few years seemed to have changed him for the better. It was only a matter of time until life would return to a semblance of normalcy.

Then in September of 1972, the Hills returned from a trip to the West Coast to meet the figure in the Hallowe'en mask. It was John's rendezvous with death. An all-out police investigation followed the murder. The authorities were anxious to end this scandalous affair, once and for all. The assassin wasn't hard to find. Tracing the murder weapon the police turned up a young member of the Houston underworld, Bobby Vandiver, and his prostitute accomplice. Vandiver confessed that for $5,000, he had accepted the contract to kill John Hill. The story he told kept detectives enthralled for six days and at the end of it he had pointed a finger at, among others, Ash Robinson. No one who knew Ash well was surprised.

According to Bobby, Ash had made it known that he would be willing to pay for the execution of his son-in-law. Ash's intermediary in the letting of the contract was a very interesting Houston woman named Lilla Paulus.

To most people, she was a somewhat eccentric but upstanding

member of the community. She lived in a respectable house and knew many of Texas' "right" people. She even led a brownie troop. What fewer people knew (and Ash was undoubtably one of them) was that Lilla had a reputation as a former prostitute and madame, that she had been married to a bookie, and that her house was considered by many to be a refuge for wandering prostitutes. She had an ear for what was going on in the underworld. With contacts on both sides of the law, she was a good choice to let a contract for the bitter millionaire.

In relatively short order, police arrested Lilla, along with the young prostitute who had accompanied Bobby Vandiver on his deadly mission. Under pressure, the young girl joined Bobby as a state's witness. The trial that followed was one of the most sensational in Texas history. The grisly stories of the previous Hill trial and the sordid backgrounds of both the defendant and the witnesses fascinated the public.

Unfortunately, Bobby had been killed prior to the trial while trying to escape from jail but his young accomplice was able to provide the jury with plenty of details about the murder and about their alleged dealings with Lilla. She could not, however, help the prosecution get enough evidence to indict Ash. Lilla was the only one who could have done that and she refused to help. In the end the trial hinged on Lilla's character and what the jury would believe of what she said.

A considerable battle ensued as the prosecution tried to slip in testimony about Lilla's past and the defense moved to block it. Finally, after days of heated discussion, the prosecution was allowed to call several witnesses, who were extremely damaging. Chief among them was Lilla's estranged daughter. She described how her mother had started her in prostitution at the age of four and had continued to make money from her until well into puberty. The jury and everybody else in the courtroom listened with open mouths. There was further damning testimony, but, in retrospect, it seems to have been her daughter's words that sealed Lilla's fate. She was found guilty and sentenced to life imprisonment. She went without saying a word about Ash Robinson.

In the furor following the verdict, Ash was asked repeatedly by the press about the nature of his involvement. He denied any

97

wrongdoing. Speculation about his role in the murder was strong and still refuses to die. After some time had passed, the Hill family even lodged a civil suit against him to try and clear the air (they lost), but nothing seems destined to answer the questions raised by this crime. John and Joan are already dead and Ash is close to dying. In all likelihood, the Hill-Robinson mystery will remain one of the most bizarre unsolved crimes of all times.

The Hall—Mills Case

THE YOUNG COUPLE STROLLED hand in hand out of the town of New Brunswick, New Jersey, and toward the farmland that surrounded it. September 16, 1922, was a pleasant fall day and the two were headed for DeRussey's Lane, the local lovers' hideaway. The young girl, a factory worker, was thrilled, but also nervous, at the prospect of being alone with her beau.

As they walked, the young man kept steering them farther and farther off the main road. Suddenly, the girl noticed two people under a crab-apple tree. Thinking she had disturbed their privacy, she stood motionless for a moment, reluctant to intrude further. Then she sensed something was wrong. Slowly she approached them. From a distance she saw that they were a man and woman lying together, the man's arm under the woman's head. Close up she saw something else. "Come here!", she cried out to her companion, "The people ain't breathin'!"

The young man hurried over. What he saw made his mouth drop open. Both people had been shot through the head, the woman, several times, once right between the eyes. Just below her chin a mass of crawling maggots marked the spot where her neck had been slit from ear to ear. Terrified, the young couple raced across the fields to the nearest farm with a telephone. Some thirty minutes later two local policemen (as they had neither patrol cars nor radios, the police actually had to hitchhike to the scene of the crime) and a newspaper reporter had begun to investigate.

Cheap stationery was scattered between the bodies and on it were written extremely passionate love letters. They were inscribed in a hand that was immature, but there was nothing immature about what they said. In language remarkably explicit for 1922, they spoke of a very torrid affair. Even more startling, a business card propped up against the dead man's foot identified him as the Reverend Edward Wheeler Hall, rector of St. John's Church in New Brunswick.

Knowing the minister's considerable stature in the community, the senior policeman left to telephone his superiors. Before the end of the day the entire community was buzzing with the news.

The reporter, too, had left but only after thoroughly studying the evidence so that he could write up the event for his paper. The crime was bizarre and it had the ingredients of a major story. As the reporter worked he wondered whether his piece would be good enough for the wire services. It was. Within hours, news of the murder began to spread across the country and a seemingly simple homicide was turned into the Hall—Mills case, one of the most celebrated unsolved murder mysteries in the history of the United States.

By the following day the female victim had also been identified. She was Eleanor Mills, wife of the church sexton and mother of two children. She was also a devoted participant in church activities and a soprano in the church choir. In the eyes of most of the church's congregation, she also seemed to be the apple of the minister's eye.

Eleanor had good reason to center her life around the church. A child bride, she had married at the age of fifteen to Jimmy Mills, a meek factory worker, and had immediately become trapped in a squalid, poverty-ridden life that left little room for any of the playfulness or lightheartedness that a young girl might hope for from life.

During her teens Eleanor buried herself in caring for her two children and housekeeping. But as her children grew older and began to need her less, Eleanor turned to romantic novels and church work, the only two outlets available to her. It was easy to find volunteer work at St. John's and she was soon able to spend as much time as she wanted to there.

At first the minister was only her friend. He was warm and understanding, often without even having to say anything. Because of the numerous church activities in which she participated, Eleanor spent many hours of the week in his company. Inevitably, the friendship grew into something quite different. As passion entered her life for the first time, Eleanor learned firsthand all the joys that had only been

100

The Reverend Hall in a pastoral pose.   (UPI photo)

Another view of the minister whose death shocked the country. (UPI photo)

hinted at in the cheap novels she read. It was heady stuff for an immature young woman who had never had an exciting moment in her life.

It was apparently heady stuff for the handsome minister, too. Reverend Hall was from Brooklyn. Born in 1881 he had attended the Episcopal seminary after graduating from college. A very personable and mild-mannered man, he had served first as a curate in New York City and then as an assistant pastor in another small New Jersey town. Finally, despite the fact that he was still a bachelor, he was given the rectorship of St. John's.

At first Reverend Hall was popular with his parishioners. The pastorate seemed to be the kind that he had always envisioned for himself and he felt at home. Soon after he arrived, he caught the eye of Frances Stevens, a member of one of the town's best families. Even though she was seven years older than Hall he felt she was a good choice to be a minister's wife and they were married.

Everything went well. The Stevens family had money (Frances stood to inherit even more) and the newlyweds took up residence in what came to be known as the Hall mansion in New Brunswick. They shared the house with Willie, Frances' eccentric brother. Then Eleanor entered the picture.

It is unlikely that, like Eleanor, the good minister had ever in his life felt real passion. The two lovers, therefore, approached their relationship with an incredible naiveté. While they were never seen in a compromising situation, the amount of time they spent together quickly gave rise to a great deal of gossip. Parishioners complained of never seeing their pastor anymore. Eleanor began to provoke hostile glances and catty comments from other women in the church.

The only people who seemed to be oblivious to the affair were Mrs. Hall and Mr. Mills. The former was a strong, prideful woman whose character, perhaps, prevented her from thinking the unthinkable. Furthermore, her husband had a demanding job that often kept him out late. She could explain his absences to herself as long as she kept wanting to explain them. Mr. Mills's professed ignorance is a bit harder to understand. Not only did his wife regularly absent herself until late in the evening, but the minister practically made himself a houseguest in the Mills's home, calling at all hours and frequently staying for dinner.

The public behavior of the lovers was so provocative, and by the standards of the time, perhaps even occasionally outrageous, that it came as no surprise to many people when the minister and his lover turned up dead.

Almost from the beginning the case was subject to the kind of mishaps that were to escalate in number as time passed. Although a guard was stationed at the murder site, so many gawkers showed up the next day that virtually every bit of evidence was picked up and handled by hundreds of people. All the grass and nearby earth was completely disturbed by the constant movement of feet. Any real search for physical evidence was thus made impossible.

The publicity that grew around the murders forced the local authorities into a prompt and thorough investigation. Unfortunately for them and for the interests of justice, nobody in the area had the resources or knowledge to conduct it. Furthermore the crime itself had been committed just over the line in Somerset County, while all of the principals were from Middlesex County. Immediately both county prosecutors vied for the case and started separate investigations. Simultaneously, big-time press coverage and pressure from state officials descended on the totally unprepared and unsophisticated local authorities. The result was a mess.

For several weeks the town was the scene of fights over jurisdictions, wild interrogations, and constant press interviews. From the very beginning the dual jurisdiction created friction. Some of the evidence was held by one sheriff, some by the other. One prosecutor ordered an autopsy, which showed that both victims had been shot to death with a 32-caliber pistol. Immediately the other prosecutor ordered his own autopsy. Subpoenas had to be issued across county lines for the bodies.

The prosecutors rivaled each other in making rash statements about progress in the case. Numerous theories were trotted out. The two had been killed by robbers; the Ku Klux Klan did it; a jealous choir singer did it; the two were killed elsewhere and then dragged to where the bodies were found. This confusion was accentuated by the colorful statements made by some of the principals and the conflicting stories told by townspeople.

As the prosecutors became more and more harried (they took to discussing their investigations with newsmen), the one in New

The Reverend's wife, Mrs. Frances Hall. (UPI photo)

A re-enactment of how Hall's body was found. Note the calling card propped against the shoe. (UPI photo)

Brunswick decided to take matters into his own hands. Doubting the story of Willie Stevens', Mrs. Hall's brother, he had detectives virtually kidnap the man and interrogate him until 2 A.M. When Willie failed to confess, the police were left to apologize to the family.

On October 8 the governor, acting under the increased pressure from the press, sent the head of the New Jersey state police down to coordinate the investigations. The next day the New Brunswick prosecutor's office announced that a charge of murder had been preferred against a local boy. The boy was one of three seen that night by the girl who had discovered the body. After police had picked him up and interrogated him, he confessed. The killing had occurred, he said, because the boys (all three) had mistaken the victims for the girl (she was a great favorite of the local boys) and her father. How one could shoot two people in the head at close range and then slit one's throat without realizing who they were was not even discussed.

The boys were popular in New Brunswick and the townspeople

did not take well to the arrests. Crowds formed and the policeman who arrested the suspect was stoned. A defense fund was set up and money collected. Across the way in Somerset County the prosecutor pooh-poohed the arrest. A few days later the girl had her father arrested and charged with incest. As the girl had already been charged with incorrigibility by her father, a judge had her locked up as well. Two days later a local policeman talked to the boy for two hours and got him to change his story. He was released and everything was back to square one.

As the investigations continued, a few things became clear. Eleanor was shot after the pastor and had put up a struggle. Mrs. Hall and Mr. Mills probably knew about the affair after all. A lot of people were unable to account for a lot of time on the night of the murders.

On October 23, some five weeks after the crime was committed, the state announced it was taking over the investigation. By now there was a regular corps of reporters covering the case and it was frequent front-page news in New York City. Within a short time, the new prosecutor came up with a surprise witness, a local hog farmer, who claimed to have seen the murders committed. Immediately the reporters dubbed her "the Pig Woman."

The Pig Woman was Jane Gibson. She raised pigs on land near the murder site and lived in a ramshackle house on the property. The night of the murder, according to the prosecutor, the Pig Woman was chasing a poacher when she observed two men and two women struggling. After a moment there were gunshots and one of the men and one of the women fell. She was sure that the woman who had done the killing had been Mrs. Hall.

Reporters immediately flocked to the Pig Woman's house, where she repeated her story, elaborating on it as she went along. Finally she was able to identify the man who had done the killing: Henry Carpender, a cousin of Mrs. Hall and a well-to-do stockbroker in New York. With that the state prosecutor began issuing subpoenas and preparing for a grand jury hearing.

The hearing itself was the biggest thing that had happened to New Brunswick in a long time. Huge crowds formed around the courthouse and speculation was intense. What was going on inside shouldn't have come as much of a surprise, though, as the growing herds of reporters had already interviewed just about everybody

107

scheduled to appear. The Pig Woman had been splashed across the front pages of the big-city tabloids described as a woman who rode a mule, had an idiot son, and feuded with another female pig farmer down the road.

It was no secret who the real targets of the investigation were; throughout the proceedings Mrs. Hall and Carpender maintained their innocence. Popular opinion in town was solidly behind the two.

Five days and sixty-seven witnesses later the grand jury refused to indict.

With this, public interest in the murders waned quickly. A few out-of-town papers kept reporters on the scene in hopes of a sudden break in the case, but most of the newsmen who had badgered locals for weeks departed. A few stories appeared now and then as local officials tried to make something of the little that was left to them, but to most people it was obvious that the case was dead.

For the next three and a half years the Hall—Mills case disappeared entirely from public view. The principals returned to what might be described as a normal life under the circumstances. Mrs. Hall traveled to Europe to recuperate. Henry Carpender continued to sell stocks. The girl who discovered the bodies went to the House of the Good Shepherd for rehabilitation and her father sat around waiting for his incest trial.

But on July 3, 1926, a petition for a marriage annulment put the case back in the spotlight. The petition was filed by the husband of the woman who had been the Halls' maid at the time of the murders. In it the husband claimed that his wife had had knowledge of the murders—specifically, that Mrs. Hall and Willie Stevens had done it. The *New York Daily Mirror* managed to get word of the petition's allegations and turned it into front-page headlines. The other tabloids quickly followed suit. In no time the governor of New Jersey felt the heat and called for a new investigation. A new special prosecutor was named and the chase began again.

Spurred on by the New York City papers, the new prosecutors took a more direct approach this time. Some three weeks after the initial *Mirror* story a warrant was issued for Mrs. Hall's arrest. This time the prosecutor's office operated with a modicum of secrecy. Evidence was not discussed with reporters and the defense lawyers were left up in the air as to the prosecution's intentions.

The "Pig Woman" has her day in court. The second time she testified from a bed.   (UPI photo)

A short time later Willie Stevens and Henry Carpender were arrested as well after a grand jury issued indictments. The stage was then set for one of the most famous trials in American history.

By this time the American and European press had taken up the Hall—Mills case with even greater fervor than they had the first time. Literally hundreds of reporters were assigned to the trial and they quickly sent hotel rates soaring. Many of the newsmen were forced to commute daily from New York. A special switchboard was set up in the courthouse basement, along with special telegraph lines.

One enterprising radio station set up a small studio across the street and assigned an athletic announcer to run back and forth from the courtroom to give live bulletins on the proceedings.

The defendants quickly assembled a high-priced team of six lawyers, and a great deal of publicity was provided as the legal adversaries locked horns in the press over the credibility of various witnesses. For weeks the prosecution hinted at new surprise witnesses and devastating testimony, while the defense lashed out at the total lack of evidence.

The trial opened on November 3, 1926, almost four years after the double murders had first shocked the country. The smalltown courtroom was packed, as were the streets outside. There was an almost carnival atmosphere of excitement and anticipation about all of it.

Because of the crush of people, the tables for the prosecution and the defense, the witness box, and the jury box were all squashed together. As many as sixteen people were seated around the defense table at various times and little space was left for walking about.

After the opening statements the prosecution presented a case that roughly paralleled the evidence presented before the first grand jury several years before. The major difference this time was the number of peripheral witnesses brought to the stand. Eager reporters gobbled up every word spoken, no matter how inconsequential, and turned it into front-page material.

In the end the prosecution's case rested on the testimony of the Pig Woman. By the time of the trial she had become seriously ill and was confined to a hospital near Newark. On the morning of her testimony she was transferred on a special cart to a waiting ambulance. Attended by two nurses and a doctor, escorted by police and followed by six cars of reporters and photographers, she was then driven very slowly to the courthouse. Once inside she was placed on a bed, from which she gave her testimony. Her memory seemed to have gotten better as she grew older. What she had to say was essentially the same except that she added some new details. Now she remembered snatches of chilling conversation and could clearly identify and implicate all three of the defendants.

The Pig Woman was upstaged in part by her mother, an even more gnarled old woman, whom the defense planted in the front row. The mother sneered at her daughter throughout her testimony and at one point began to call her a liar.

The testimony and cross-examinations went on for four front-page weeks. In the end, despite all the publicity, it became obvious that the prosecution had virtually nothing besides the somewhat dubious word of the Pig Woman. Careful reporters noticed signs of boredom in the jury and the chief prosecutor began to speak hostilely of the jurors and the town.

On Friday, December 3, the summations were finished and the jury went out. A little over four and a half hours later they were back with a verdict: not guilty.

Interest in the case died quickly after the verdict. For several weeks the defendants were tied up in legal maneuvering, but before long the Hall—Mills case disappeared from the front pages, never more to return. Occasionally over the years some new story or allegation would pop up, but each was always proved false. The defendants returned to a more or less normal life and the newspapers turned to new and more sensational crimes to sell their product.

What really happened that night under the crab-apple tree? About all that is certain are the facts of the murders themselves. Somebody shot both the reverend and the choir singer, somebody cut her throat. The motive seems obviously to have been the illicit affair.

Clearly Mrs. Hall and her relatives had a motive for murder. And because the trial testimony certainly didn't eliminate them as suspects it is still distinctly possible that either Mrs. Hall or others could have hired someone to do the killing. It is also not unreasonable to suspect the Ku Klux Klan. The Klan, which was strong in rural New Jersey in the late twenties, was notorious for taking violent action to punish "sins against morality." The double deaths on DeRussey Lane may have been another chapter in the Klan's violent history. Nobody knows. Despite the hundreds of thousands of words written in newspapers, magazines, and books, the truth about what happened that dark night in 1922 will be unknown forever.

A National Outrage

THE YOUNG SUBMARINE OFFICER rushed up the steps and into the living room of his modest Honolulu home. On the sofa his wife sat dressed in pajamas and a robe. She was sobbing hysterically. One glance was enough to cut through the evening's alcoholic intake and let Lieutenant Thomas Massie know that something was very wrong. His pretty young wife's eyes were red and swollen. Her lips were puffy and there was a large bruise on her right cheek. Blood trickled from her nose and mouth.

Tommie pulled her into his arms and comforted her as she tried to tell him what had happened. What she had to say was very ugly. Some half dozen Hawaiians had abducted her, she said, taken her to a remote place, beaten her, and raped her repeatedly. "I want to die," she cried. "Why didn't they kill me?"

A mass rape is no longer a crime that attracts national attention. But in 1931, in a peaceful island community so free of racial problems and sexual assault that it was termed "a paradise," such an incident was shocking beyond belief. In mainland America, where lynch law still ruled in rural areas and where racism was still constitutional, such an incident involving the U.S. Navy near Presidential election time was potential dynamite. When Thalia Massie lay sobbing on her sofa she thought that she had seen the worst suffering of her life. Little did she know that the passions and wild accusations she was about to unleash would lead to riots, beatings, and ultimately to murder. The populations of both the islands and the mainland would be convulsed, careers would be changed, and she herself

113

Thomas and Thalia Massie on their wedding day. (UPI photo)

would be ruined for life, a hopeless emotional case whose only wish would be for an early death.

The Hawaii of 1931 bore little resemblance to the fiftieth state today. Most of the natural beauty was the same (Waikiki Beach, however, did not exist. The plans to transform a swamp into a tourist beach had not yet been approved), but the islands' population and life were very different. More than three-fourths of the people living on the islands were oriental. A majority of these were not natives but poor Japanese laborers imported to do farm work. Significant efforts to organize these ethnic groups had not begun in 1931 and to a certain extent they constituted a kind of silent majority. There were racial tensions—certainly no group likes being poor—but the generally easy atmosphere of Hawaii seemed to tranquilize everyone. Even sexual problems were minimized by this atmosphere. On the one hand, the Japanese had very rigid attitudes toward the subject. On the other, the remnants of the original Hawaiians had, despite long efforts by missionaries, a very take-it-as-it-comes attitude about sex. Forcible rape was almost unheard of because force was never required.

The lives of the whites in Hawaii were centered around the two main economic activities on the island, agriculture and the Navy. The sugar-cane and pineapple empires were already well established by 1931, as were the five powerful import-export companies that virtually ran the rest of the territory (the islands were then ruled by a presidentially appointed governor). The Navy, with its enormous base at Pearl Harbor, provided the other big cash input. Tourism, today the backbone of the island economy, was still in its infancy.

To Tommie Massie and his fellow navy men, Hawaii was a choice duty station. The surroundings were luxurious and life was inexpensive. Tommie loved his life in the service. He reveled in the close camaraderie of the submariners and he spent most of his time drinking and playing practical jokes with his fellow officers.

Hawaii was not such a paradise to his wife. Thalia was the daughter of a high-bred eastern family. Her mother, Mrs. Grace Fortescu, lived in luxury on Long Island. Thalia had married young and it had taken her a while to realize that the boisterous, often crude Navy life was the wrong one for her. Her marriage was in trouble and she didn't know what to do about it.

115

Thalia as a submariner's wife. (UPI photo)

The night of the attack she had reluctantly attended a submariners' party. Thalia and Tommie had fallen out almost as soon as they arrived. Thalia, furious, sat upstairs with acquaintances. Finally, some time shortly before midnight, she walked off by herself. What happened to her on that walk has remained a matter of speculation to this day.

As soon as Tommie had heard his wife's story he dialed the police and within a few minutes a patrol car had arrived at their house. A detective immediately questioned Thalia. She repeated the story she had told her husband. How did you know that the assailants were Hawaiian?, she was asked. Because of the way they spoke, she answered. Did you see the license plate? No, I did not, but I do remember that the car was a convertible and that the top was ripped. These answers would prove fateful.

Earlier in the evening a Hawaiian woman had had a run-in with a car full of local boys. The police knew the license number of that car and immediately assumed that the same young men were probably responsible for both incidents.

The police were as stunned as everybody else. Assaults did occur, if infrequently, but rape of a white woman by orientals was unheard of. As the authorities rushed to investigate, a series of events rapidly unfolded that would shroud the entire case in mystery forever.

Thalia was taken to the hospital, where she was given a thorough internal examination. The doctor found no evidence of rape, although he refused to rule out the possibility absolutely. While Thalia was in the hospital she found herself by a window just above a parked police car. The car's radio was turned up to full volume to enable the officer accompanying Thalia to hear. Three separate times while Thalia listened, the police dispatcher announced the license number of the vehicle being sought in the other assault. When Thalia's medical examination was completed she was taken to police headquarters for further questioning.

In the meantime police had traced the car and arrested twenty-four-year-old Horace Ida, a Japanese-American. Like many educated boys of his class and background he had little to do and not too much to look forward to. In the Hawaii of 1931 this attitude translated itself into activities such as surfing, hanging out, and drinking.

The night of the incident Ida had borrowed his sister's car and had driven around with friends, traveling back and forth between a private party and a public dance. Several different acquaintances had shared the car during the evening but police were finally able to trace four of them: two Hawaiians, a Chinese-American, and another Japanese-American. Two of the five had minor police records.

In rapid succession the five were taken before Thalia, who identified two of them as her assailants. (This was done without a lineup; the suspects were simply brought in by themselves.) At the same time Thalia said she could now remember the license plate. It turned out to be virtually the same number she had heard over the police radio.

Thalia then identified the car, despite the fact that the top had no rip in it. The underwear of all five defendants as well as the victim's was examined, but no signs of semen could be found. Furthermore, witnesses existed who could account for virtually all the defendants' time and activities including the assault on the Hawaiian woman until shortly before the crime. The account of the witnesses left no time for the assault on Thalia. Furthermore, testimony from each of the defendants, taken before they could speak to each other, corroborated their alibis.

Normally any prosecutor faced with a case so weak would never go to court. But within a few days of the attack on Thalia, events outside normal legal channels pushed the entire affair down the road toward tragedy.

The local Navy commander had originally adopted a hands-off attitude toward the case. Admiral Stirling was a Southerner and a racist, but he was also responsible for Navy affairs on the island and he was fearful of repercussions if the affair was not handled quickly and quietly. Keeping Washington and the national press ignorant of the affair, he pressed the local authorities for a speedy trial of the five. At the same time he took precautions (canceling leave among other things) to prevent vigilante action by Navy personnel.

A few weeks after the assault, Thalia's mother arrived. Mrs. Fortescu was an elegant, dominating woman who overwhelmed most of the people she met. She became highly indignant as soon as she learned the details of what had (allegedly) happened to her daughter, and began to use every resource at her disposal to press for a trial. And as a woman with strong political and economic connections in the East, her resources were formidable. A short time after Mrs. Fortescu's arrival, an indictment of the five was handed up.

Although sentiment among Navy personnel was in favor of hanging, the defense attorneys were extremely confident. The prosecution could not even prove a rape had been committed, let alone the identity of the perpetrators. This confidence proved justified because, after a very emotional trial, the racially mixed jury was unable to come to a verdict and a mistrial was ordered. The result was explosive.

Navy personnel in Hawaii had always looked upon themselves as a class apart and above the racially mixed islanders. When news of the mistrial reached the base, talk of vigilante action spread like wildfire. For the first few days it was mostly just talk, but within a short while plans were formed. One group planned to steal gasoline and burn down the Japanese section of Honolulu, which was built mainly of wood and paper. Another group planned a military invasion by three thousand seamen. This group went so far as to outfit a vehicle with machine guns and send it downtown, but the plan came to nothing.

The Saturday after the verdict thousands of Navy men swarmed through downtown Honolulu and several fights broke out. At the same time a group of sailors abducted Horace Ida, took him off into the country, and beat him until he passed out. With that, all hell broke loose.

A Marine detachment was ordered into the city to maintain order. News of the events now reached Washington, both through highly biased Navy news releases and via the press. The gist of both laid the blame for everything on the local population. Hawaii was described as unsafe for white women and it was suggested that plans for fleet maneuvers that called for stops in the islands be changed.

Admiral Stirling and others pressed for a new trial and a massive reorganization of the police force. (During the trial it had become obvious that many of the policemen sympathized more with the defendants than the prosecution. Given the lack of evidence and the racial pressure exerted by the Navy, this was hardly surprising.)

The governor managed to effect the reorganization but he was very reluctant to move for a retrial. The case was no stronger than it had been before. A conviction appeared impossible and even unwarranted. Moreover the local population was becoming indignant at what it perceived as harassment, bigotry, and illegal intervention by the Navy in local affairs.

It was in this setting that Mrs. Fortescu decided to take matters into her own hands. She had come to realize that a conviction would be impossible without a confession by at least one of the assailants. Blinded by hate, and by her loyalty to her daughter, she became determined to get that confession.

Pressing Tommie Massie into service (Tommie was in a desperate emotional condition by this time), she decided to kidnap one of the defendants and force a confession out of him at gunpoint. To provide the brawn, Mrs. Fortescu enlisted a sailor the navy had provided as a bodyguard for her. He brought along one of his friends. Both were fleet boxers and very strong men.

Joseph Kahahawai, a huge, hulking man quick with his fists, was selected as the target. Kahahawai was the suspect who had hit the Hawaiian woman. No one knows exactly why the conspirators chose him.

One month after the verdict that set the defendants free, Mrs. Fortescu, Tommie Massie, and the two sailors kidnapped Kahahawai on the steps of the Judiciary Building where the Hawaiian was reporting as required by his probation on another charge. A hastily faked subpoena was used to ensure his cooperation.

Mrs. Fortescu proved to a bungling criminal. A close friend of Kahahawai's witnessed the abduction and promptly reported it to the police, complete with the license number of the car involved.

The police broadcast an alert. About an hour and a half later, after a short chase, the car was stopped near some cliffs overlooking the sea. Mrs. Fortescu, Tommie Massie, and one of the seamen got out of the car. In the back seat the policemen found the body of Joseph Kahahawai. He was dead, shot once through the chest.

While the police escorted the three downtown, other officers swarmed over the Fortescu house. There they found the other seaman, two pistols, and a shell casing. A guest bedroom was in total disarray, the door almost completely torn off its hinges. The bathroom showed signs of having been hastily cleaned. Under the sink detectives found two buttons that turned out to be from Kahahawai's undershorts.

120

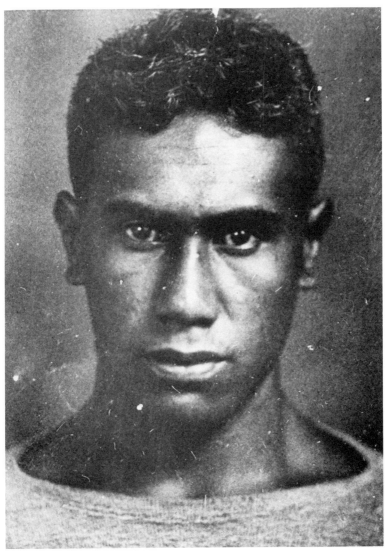

Joe Kahahawai—suspect or scapegoat?   (UPI photo)

A now-enraged governor immediately pressed for and quickly received murder indictments on all four. The case seemed open and shut. Because of the islanders' hostile feelings about the rape trial, there seemed little doubt of the outcome of this trial. But this would be no ordinary proceeding. On the very day of the crime, the first bit of outside intervention occurred. It was a small taste of what was to come.

Because of the Navy's special influence in the islands, servicemen were normally kept in military custody. Although, technically, murder suspects were under local jurisdiction, and Mrs. Fortescu was clearly under local jurisdiction, there was no precedent for the current situation.

Admiral Stirling quickly stepped in and proposed that the Navy retain custody of the prisoners, with the understanding that they would be handed over at the will of the Hawaiian authorities. A reluctant attorney general accepted. The four were whisked away after the indictment proceedings and housed on a converted cruiser. As soon as the hullabaloo died down they were given free run of the base.

Anger coursed through the local population. Jeering crowds had formed when the indictments were handed up, and there was a lot of angry talk throughout the nonwhite neighborhoods. The local newspapers covered the story in great detail, and few came away from reading the press without a sense of indignation and horror.

On the mainland, however, a very different picture was being painted. Grace Fortescu had a lot of influential friends, and to them the case was quite simple. As a Hearst newspaper headlined it, it was "The Honor Slaying."

The first day of "imprisonment," Mrs. Fortescu literally received a boatload of flowers. Telegrams poured in from newspaper owners, politicians, and socialites across the nation offering sympathy and support.

Overnight the American press took up the "cause." Conveniently ignoring the facts, newspapers across the country began to decry "the atmosphere of lawlessness and rape that gripped the islands" and "forced decent white folks to take up arms to protect the honor of their women." Alleged atrocity stories (all false) of other rapes and assaults were circulated in print. Editorials called on "decent folk" to rise up and demand "martial law" for a place where "degenerate natives and half-whites lie in wait for white women driving by."

The Navy quickly took up the hue and cry. Admiral Stirling had already told the governor that the local atmosphere was to blame for the murder. The higher authorities quickly took up his position. The Chief of Naval Operations: "American men will not stand for the violation of their women under any circumstances. For this crime they have taken the matter into their own hands repeatedly when they have felt that the law has failed to do justice."

Maneuvers were canceled and in Congress (remember an election was coming up) similar cries were taken up.

In the teeth of all this fury the local authorities went ahead with preparations for the trial. The prosecutors were confident that they had a strong case. Public opinion was with them and the entire nonwhite population on the island was looking forward to the trial.

The defendants were a lot less happy. At first they had believed that the grand jury would fail to indict. When the indictment was handed up and the seriousness of their situation was made apparent, Mrs. Fortescu began, through her friends, to search for a suitable defense counsel. She wanted the best man possible. Her friends came up with Clarence Darrow.

To this day no one is sure why Darrow took the case. One of the main factors may have been money. He had been hit hard by the Depression and was in serious financial trouble. The $30,000 he asked as a fee would go a long way for the seventy-five year old man.

Darrow quickly added a special notoriety to the case. Traveling to the West Coast by train, the famous lawyer was besieged by reporters at every stop. Careful not to reveal any defense strategy, he nevertheless, day by day, gave out colorful tidbits that kept the press clamor alive. His arrival in Honolulu was an even bigger event. By now the case had received so much national publicity that correspondents from all over the country were in Hawaii.

No amount of publicity could alter the facts of the crime, however, and many doubted that even Darrow could get the accused off. The lawyer had weighed the situation carefully and had decided on a defense tactic that was brand new in 1932—temporary insanity.

The trial opened much as expected. A mixed jury was selected,

123

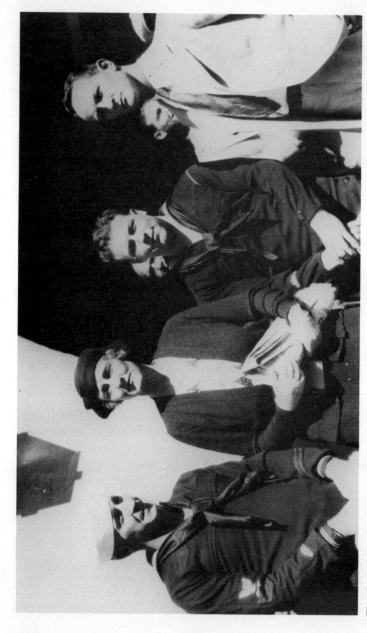

The four defendants (Seaman Jones, Mrs. Grace Fortescu, Seaman Lord and Tommie Massie) in Hawaii's most famous trial. (UPI photo)

consisting of five whites, three Europeans, three Chinese, and one juror of mixed ancestry. The whites were local people and by now their employers (the powerful export firms) had come out openly for conviction. Darrow considered the jury a disaster for the defense and he told his assistant, "From now on we'll try the case in the press."

The prosecution then presented its witnesses who seemed to fix the blame irrefutably. Darrow chose to ignore the prosecution testimony and bore in on the issue of insanity. He carefully implied, without stating it, that Tommie Massie had fired the fatal shot. (The state had never determined what really happened inside the house.) The famed attorney of the Scopes trial then attempted to show that the rape had put Massie under such pressure that it had caused a blackout, or temporary insanity.

The jury deliberated for more than two days before finding the defendants guilty of manslaughter. In Hawaii the verdict was well received. On the mainland it caused an explosion. The day after the verdict, headlines and editorials across the country blasted the trial and everyone connected with the prosecution. The four defendants were acclaimed crusaders, righteous defenders of white womanhood scurrilously abused by a corrupt colored population.

By the time Congress met on the following Monday (the verdict came on Friday), senators and representatives alike were calling for a presidential pardon and federal intervention. When it was pointed out that the president had no power to pardon in such a case, bills were introduced to give him that authority.

Back on the islands the governor agonized over what to do. The four defendants had each been sentenced to ten years in jail. The civilian populace was happy with the sentence. Any reversal of the verdict by the governor could cause severe domestic troubles. On the other hand the Navy and the press were putting heavy pressure on the territory. A military boycott had already damaged the local economy. And threats of further cancellations of maneuvers and possible federal intervention were left hanging.

Seeking a workable compromise, the governor called Darrow to his residence for a conference. In the middle of their meeting the governor received a call from the president. That did it.

Two days later the governor delivered what was one of the most curious and controversial sentencing agreements in American judicial

125

history. Speaking before the national press the governor announced that although each of the defendants had been sentenced to ten years imprisonment, he was commuting the sentences to one hour to be served in his chambers. With that the defendants were freed.

Part of the agreement between Darrow and the governor called for Thalia Massie's quick and permanent departure from the island, which occurred a few days later. No one knows what caused the young wife's change of heart about pressing for a new trial, but part of it is ascribed to conversations with her gynecologist. The doctor later said, "If I had . . . to tell everything I knew . . . it would have made monkeys out of everybody."

In time the uproar over the case died down and most people forgot it. Hawaii returned to the business of growth that would ultimately mark it for statehood.

Both seamen remained in the submarine service and eventually rose to the rank of chief petty officer. Two years after the trial, Thalia and Tommie were divorced. Tommie went on to remarry, and left the Navy to enter business.

The trauma of what had happened to her remained with Thalia for the rest of her life. For several years after her divorce she bounced back and forth from suicide attempts to hospital confinements. She remarried and seemed to lead a normal life. Then on July 3, 1963, she was found dead, a suicide by barbiturates.

Was Thalia Massie in fact raped? Who beat her up? What went on in the Fortescu house that fatal afternoon? Who really killed Joseph Kahahawai? These are questions that may never be answered.

FANCY
CLOTHES AND
FAST LIVING

Death strikes all of us, but for those who choose a fast life it often comes in strange guises. Sexual attractiveness, fame, and wealth are no protection against the Grim Reaper, as these people suddenly found out.

Vivian Gordon

THE BODY WAS THAT of a very attractive, fortyish redhead. Everything about her bespoke a stylish sexuality. Her legs were long and firm, her face still lovely, almost haunting. She was dressed in a Paris-made black velvet dress, silk underwear, and sheer stockings. Her name was Vivian Gordon and she was dead.

Vivian's body was found early on February 26, 1931, just a few hours before she was scheduled to testify before a state commission investigating police corruption. In the furor that followed her death and the investigation that ensued, her name became synonymous with an ever-growing story of prostitution, wild parties, blackmail, and violence. Miss Gordon was no ordinary girl, and in the publicity surrounding her demise her true role as Broadway courtesan, high-class madame, and full-scale extortionist became public knowledge.

Vivian was the daughter of John Franklin, former warden of the Illinois State Penitentiary in Joliet. Her upbringing had been strict and tightly supervised. Then as a teen-ager she was sent away to a convent school in Canada. Vivian did not fit into this tight mold; when she was eighteen she rebelled. Running away from the convent, she took up her first love, acting. For a while she was a theater gypsy, touring around the country with second-rate theatrical companies. During this period she met and married John Bischoff. Always restless, and despite the birth of a daughter (Benita), she soon tired of Bischoff and the role of a wife. In 1921 she left him, taking her daughter with her to New York.

While there Vivian struggled hard dabbling in acting and modeling but never getting very far. Finally she turned to prostitution and

131

there found a calling that suited her. At first she worked the streets, often bringing clients back to the room she shared with her daughter. Then in 1923 Vivian was arrested on a morals charge and sent to the state prison at Bedford. Her daughter was taken from her and sent to live with a grandmother in New Jersey.

Prison did little but harden Vivian. When she returned to the city from Bedford she made a determined drive to establish herself as a big-name madame. In time she developed a network of more than fifty beautiful girls. Many of them worked in nightclubs, where they met men from out of town with a lot of money. Other clients came from the network of spotters that Vivian maintained in influential places. She also kept close contact with the underworld and with political figures and was always ready to provide women for a private party or for a night on the town.

Wherever Vivian's girls went, her eyes and ears went too, for the one-time convent student was also deeply involved in blackmail. Several of her girls later testified that they were always instructed to learn the name and position of anyone they dallied with. In most cases Vivian quickly turned this information to advantage through extortion. Over the years, her victims numbered in the hundreds.

New York in the 1920s (the Prohibition era) was a thoroughly corrupt city run by the all-powerful Tammany Hall machine. Judgeships were bought and sold like automobiles. Elections were rigged. Police were often as not on the take. This aura of corruption was hardly new to the city. What was new in the early 1930s, however, was signs of rebellion against this system.

In the two years preceding Vivian's death, chicanery had brought down several powerful judges and other public figures and the police were being publicly questioned by the press. In 1931, a state commission was set up to investigate police corruption in the city. It put a lot of pressure on local officials.

Out of motives that no one will ever know for sure, Vivian Gordon offered to testify before the commission. She was scheduled to appear at 10 A.M. on the morning of February 26. As we know, she never made it.

Her body was found near the side of a park road in the Bronx. She was fully clothed and showed no disfigurement except for the

Vivian Gordon.   (UPI photo)

bruises on her neck caused by the length of dirty clothesline that had strangled her to death.

The autopsy showed that she had died sometime during the night. She had eaten a large meal earlier in the evening and had finished it off with a lot of whiskey. There were no signs of rape.

The initial police investigation revealed that she had been wearing a $585 wristwatch, a $1,200 ring, and an $1,800 fur coat earlier in the evening. This information started the cops off on the theory that she had been killed by robbers. On the other hand, the majority of the public speculated that she had been taken for a ride by the police.

It didn't take long for news of the murder to leak out. Once the state commission learned of the death of their witness they put pressure on the city to solve the crime. The chief of police took drastic action to try to save face. His position and his pension were threatened by the mounting publicity. As he put it to the press, "Until this case is cleared up, every policeman in New York has a smudge on his shield!"

For 134 days a task force of detectives tried to prove that Vivian had been killed by robbers or by one of her blackmail victims. A search of her apartment had turned up a diary and a ledger listing her call girls and some five hundred prominent men who were actual or prospective extortion victims. Police tackled all the names on the list. Detectives were sent around the country to check out alibis. Call girls were brought in and grilled.

When this turned up nothing, and as the pressure grew, the police reluctantly turned to investigating her past and her diary.

It was finally learned that Vivian had planned to testify about the original arrest that had sent her to Bedford. A search of old records showed that the arrest had been set up by her husband to gain custody of the daughter. The police immediately suspected that Vivian's testimony may have been primarily an attempt to blackmail or gain revenge on her husband.

On his own John Bischoff came to New York for questioning and provided a convincing story. He also demonstrated that the divorce had been caused by personal incompatibility. He made no mention of vice. The detective in that case, who had been in the employ of the husband, likewise had an alibi. He had been off on a six-day cruise to

Bermuda at the time of the murder. (Vivian's claim of a frame-up may have been true, however. The detective was brought up on an internal police investigation a short time later. He was asked to explain how his bank account came to contain $35,800 when he made a salary of $3,000. He refused to answer and was dismissed.)

The police now turned to investigating two names which figured prominently in Vivian's diary. One of these men was an underworld lawyer named John Radeloff. It was quickly established that the handsome, dark-haired Radeloff was not only the victim's lawyer, but also her financial adviser and former lover. After a time Radeloff cooled towards Vivian, which deeply hurt her. The police received a report that when Radeloff had threatened to move his things out of her apartment, she in turn had threatened to tell his wife about their relationship. A furious Radeloff was then alleged to have warned Vivian that he had someone who could do her in.

That someone was a repulsive-looking hood called Chowderhead Cohen. Chowderhead was a former safecracker whose real name was Sam. His nickname came from a huge head that expanded from normal size at the top to a set of enormous jowls at the bottom. Chowderhead was a big man and often complained that he had to starve himself to keep his weight down to 280 pounds.

Police investigated both Radeloff and Chowderhead thoroughly and learned that the latter had also served as an enforcer for Vivian, but both suspects had airtight alibis for the time of the murder and police abandoned them as suspects (a bit prematurely, as we shall see).

In going through Vivian's diary the detectives came across an entry that indicated she had lent $1,500 to a man named Charles Reuben. Penciled after his name were the initials O-S-L-O.

The police searched shipping records and finally spotted a Charles Reuben listed on a voyage of the superliner *Berengaria*. The destination of the *Berengaria* was Scandinavia. The date was July 20, 1929. Reuben was listed as having shared a cabin with two other men.

The police took Reuben's passport application and had a handwriting expert compare it with those of other figures in the case. After several days the expert announced that the handwriting was that of Harry Stein.

135

Harry Stein had also been mentioned in the diary. Like Chowderhead, he had served for a while as an enforcer for Vivian. During that period he had also been her friend.

A police investigation revealed two other items: that Stein was a client of lawyer John Radeloff and that Stein had served time in Sing Sing for strangling a woman to death.

This lead looked better and better. In a short time the authorities had located Stein and put him under round-the-clock surveillance, tapping his phone as well. Within a short time they turned up a friend of Stein's named Sam Greenberg. Greenberg was a con man and a frequent lunch companion of Stein's. Police informants suspected that the two had been involved in several shady dealings together.

About the same time, police investigating the cruise to Scandinavia determined that Stein had been accompanied on the trip by both Greenberg and another underworlder named Harry Schlitten.

Then another piece of information popped up that seemed to clinch the case. Within an hour of the murder Stein had approached a fur jobber and asked him to sell a fur coat and some jewelry. The jobber had taken the coat and jewelry to his connections for an appraisal. The deal had fallen through because of the murder publicity. The items that Stein had offered were the items worn by Vivian Gordon.

Police also learned that the night of the murder Harry Schlitten and another man had rented a Cadillac limousine, returning it early the next day.

Armed with this information the police obtained warrants and arrested Stein, Greenberg, and Schlitten. At first the suspects were closemouthed. But the police applied considerable pressure (they were under a lot of pressure themselves) and finally broke Schlitten.

The next day the police commissioner gave out the following account of what happened:

At a casual get-together with Schlitten, Stein broached the subject of Vivian Gordon and her blackmail racket. "If I don't put a certain party away," Stein allegedly said, "a friend of mine is going to end up in jail." Stein then asked Schlitten to give him a hand and help him get a limousine in which to do the killing.

The night of the murder Schlitten and Greenberg drove the

Cadillac to the Bronx and waited at a prearranged corner. Stein showed up a bit later with Vivian in a cab. He had allegedly lured Vivian there with a tip that Greenberg had a quarter of a million dollars in stolen diamonds to sell. Stein and Vivian joined Greenberg in the back seat while Schlitten drove.

As soon as the car was in motion Stein pulled out a length of clothesline, made it into a noose, and slipped it over Vivian's head. Together the two men shoved her to the floor and put their feet on top of her while Stein pulled on the noose. Schlitten said he heard a short struggle in the back seat and when he turned around the woman was dead. He added, "She only cackled once."

After confessing, Schlitten led police to the spot where one of Vivian's shoes had been tossed out after the murder (the shoe had apparently fallen off in the car when the body was dumped). Police immediately found the shoe.

Greenberg and Stein went on trial in June. Schlitten had been given immunity in exchange for his testimony. The trial opened amid a great deal of publicity. One after another the prosecution witnesses came to the stand and gave their stories. The case they made was very strong.

Stein and Greenberg were defended by the famous Samuel Leibowitz. Leibowitz' main tactic was to discredit Schlitten, the chief prosecution witness. In a tough cross-examination, Leibowitz dragged out all of Schlitten's sordid past. Schlitten was forced to admit that he was a friend of various thugs and murderers; that he made his money dealing illegal poker games and running an afterhours club; and that he had participated in an armored-car holdup. He also admitted he "went out to murder for money." Leibowitz also produced alibis for the two defendants. Greenberg's was particularly colorful. He claimed that he spent the evening at home participating in a religious ceremony.

Leibowitz's tactics paid off. Contrary to everybody's expectations, the jury returned a verdict of not guilty.

The acquittals were, for all practical purposes, the official end of the Vivian Gordon case. There have been no new leads, and the uncertainty concerning what really happened lingers to this day.

The trial did leave a trail of misfortune, however. The first victim of it was Vivian's sixteen-year-old daughter, who committed suicide because she "could not bear the shame." In 1950 the police detective who had arrested Vivian on the morals charge shot himself to death in his Queens home. And finally in 1955, Harry Stein was electrocuted in Sing Sing for his part in a stickup-murder.

William Desmond Taylor

WILLIAM DESMOND TAYLOR was once one of the best-known directors in movies. In the years between 1918 and 1922 Taylor was for many people the symbol of flashy, decadent living that would soon make Hollywood famous around the world. He drove expensive sports cars and wore custom-made clothes. He had a fabulous mansion and partied with some of the cinema's most gorgeous women. He also had a mysterious past. At the beginning of 1922 he appeared to be a man with everything, money, fame, and women. By the morning of February 2, 1922, he was dead and his name became linked forever, not with the immortal glamour of the silver screen, but with one of the most notorious murder mysteries of our times.

Taylor was born in Ireland, the son of a major in the British Army. His name at birth was William Cunningham Deane-Tanner. William was brought up in a military environment and for most of his childhood was groomed to be an officer. But little Willie had other ideas and soon displayed a strong desire to get into the theater.

Faced with the rebelliousness of his son (whose eyesight was so bad that he failed the army physical), the major sent William and his younger brother off to a new life in the United States. William bounced around the country for a while, but eventually his strict upbringing made itself felt and he settled down to a prestigious position as vice-president of the exclusive English Antique Shop in New York. William acquired a conservative wardrobe and began associating with the kind of people who inhabit the world of wealth.

In 1901 he married a former showgirl and set up residence in the then very exclusive town of Larchmont, New York. He became a

William Desmond Taylor as director.   (UPI photo)

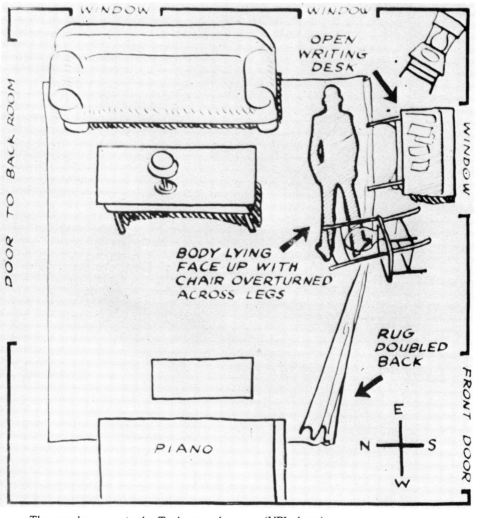

The murder scene in the Taylor townhouse. (UPI photo)

member of the yacht club and a figure in local politics. His wife, too, settled comfortably into the stability and security of upper-class suburban life. In 1903 they had a daughter, Ethel Daisy, and William seemed destined for the kind of staid, comfortable life that every businessman dreams of.

William may have been one of the most misunderstood people in modern times. For over eight years he led this routine, conformist life and everyone that knew him believed him to be happy. He wasn't. One day in 1908 he calmly went out to lunch and never came back.

William had a terrible lust for adventure that had been bottled up ever since his childhood. Freed from restraint, he set out to redo his life and make up for lost time. First he sought his fortunes in the goldfields. He struck out in Colorado, then moved to Montana and finally the Klondike. When he finally gave up on prospecting he turned to the one love of his life—theater. After a short stint with a theatrical company in Alaska he set out for Hollywood and the infant movie industry. He also changed his name. From now on the world would know him as William Desmond Taylor.

William was a gifted talker and shortly after his arrival in Tinseltown he managed to obtain a job as director of a movie serial (à la Pearl White) called *The Diamond from the Sky*. He also was an actor and very quickly built up not only a growing career for himself, but also an image as one of Hollywood's leading playboys. He never scrimped on spending and from the beginning displayed a real style with fancy clothes and fast cars. He inevitably attracted a lot of women and, as his career grew, he became a man to know. This rapid career rise almost brought him to grief.

In the years since William disappeared from New York, his wife had become reconciled to his absence. Believing him to be dead, she filed for divorce in 1912 and went about leading her conservative life.

A few years after the divorce the wife took her daughter to the movies. The two sat comfortably in the theater munching popcorn until the leading man appeared on the screen. Suddenly the wife stood up. "Why, Ethel Daisy. That's your father!" she screamed. She was very upset and made attempts to locate William and get what she felt was her due. Unfortunately for her she had already obtained a divorce and didn't have much ground left to stand on.

Taylor took a year out for military service during World War I, but

Taylor displaying his matinée-idol machismo.   (UPI photo)

Mary Miles Mintner—her mother packed a .38.   (UPI photo)

despite his love of adventure army life disagreed with him. Before long he was back in Hollywood directing movies. Taylor was good and in no time he had become not only well known to the public but also respected by his peers, and he was elected to the presidency of the Motion Picture Directors' Society.

By now William lived in a lavish home on South Alvarado Street, deep in celebrity country. The dwelling was Spanish stucco and to go with his fancy car and expensive wardrobe he kept a manservant (days only—in the evening he kept women). His first butler was an impeccable-looking Englishman named Edward Sands. Sands was impeccable in looks only. One day while William was away on a trip he forged some checks, pawned his master's jewelry, went wild with his charge accounts, wrecked both cars, and stole all his custom-made clothes.

To replace him, the director obtained a docile black butler named Henry Peavey. Peavey spoke with a high-pitched voice and did needlepoint in his spare time.

The night of the murder found William at home with Peavey and actress Mabel Normand. Normand was at the time one of the nation's favorite comic actresses and she doted on William.

Peavey left at 7:30 P.M. and Mabel departed a few minutes later with a volume of Nietzsche under her arm. William liked his women well read and always gave them little tidbits to chew on.

About thirty minutes after she left, neighbors heard what sounded like a shot. Nobody paid much attention, thinking it to be a automobile backfire. One neighbor who did look out a bit later claimed to have seen a man, or a woman dressed like a man, sneaking away from the Taylor home.

The following morning Peavey returned to work and found the body of his employer stretched out on the living-room floor. Taylor's arms were by his side and his feet together, giving the impression that he was lying at attention. Only the dried blood by his mouth betrayed that he was dead.

Screaming in his falsetto voice Peavey ran outside looking for help. A passing doctor was called in and he promptly labeled William a victim of gastric hemorrhage. A few minutes later the police arrived. They rolled the body over and found a 38-caliber bullet hole in the director's back.

Mary posing as a sweet young thing.   (UPI photo)

One of the neighbors, an actress herself, had kept an eye on Taylor's nighttime frolics and knew who was who. She quickly called Mabel and another beauty named Mary Miles Minter. Mary was a lot newer than Mabel and was still building her career. She specialized in ingenue roles and was being groomed to compete with Mary Pickford.

The police were stymied from the start. The killer had left no clues to his/her identity or motive. A careful search of William's bedroom turned up a lot of women's lingerie and a series of love letters. One written by Mabel was addressed to "Dearest Daddy" and signed "Blessed Baby." Another from Mary was filled with professions of love.

With nothing else to go on, the police began exploring the director's love life. Mabel was quickly eliminated as a suspect but at the beginning they were suspicious of Mary. Or rather of her mother.

Mary lived with her mother and the situation was not healthy. A maid revealed that Mary's mother was bitterly opposed to her daughter's affair with William and had threatened to do something about it. It also turned out that the kindly mother packed a .38 on occasion.

Little Mary then turned around and accused her mother of being jealous and wanting William for herself. Despite this, the police were unable to build a case against the mother and eventually they dropped that lead. Although her mother's innocence was proven, Mary found the whole experience disastrous. After all the nationwide publicity about her affair (including descriptions of her undies and nightgowns), she found it hard to get film roles as a sweet young thing. For all practical purposes her acting career came to an end.

The police continued the investigation for quite some time. They looked for the English butler. They quizzed all the girl friends. They looked for any possibility of blackmail. They found nothing.

The only motive for the killing that ever seemed a real possibility revolved around drugs. Despite his wild life-style Taylor was violently opposed to drugs. Cocaine and marijuana were the rage at the time among many show-business people and had been involved in a series of scandals that included that surrounding Fatty Arbuckle. At one point Taylor had gone to the police and fingered a lot of people, resulting in a series of arrests, primarily of dope dealers. The

147

homicide detectives made a thorough check of every narcotics lead they had, but no evidence of a vengeance rub-out could be discovered.

In the end the police were left with little more than the facts of the director's death. No motive and no suspect has ever been found.

Taylor was buried in a ceremony befitting his adventurous life. A lot of people shed tears at his passing, though few today remember the sensational surroundings of his death, the secret of which lies buried with him and always will.

Starr Faithfull

STARR FAITHFULL WAS a beautiful young woman and the life she led seemed to most to be sinful, sensual, and happy. She was constantly in the company of men and more than once was caught in a compromising situation. She loved a drink and carried a flask of martinis around when she went out on the town. To many women she was symbolic of the evil but exciting life they secretly aspired to.

On the night of June 8, 1931, Starr's body was found lying on a Long Island beach clad only in a silk dress. In the months that followed, the circumstances surrounding her death catapulted her into posthumous national celebrity. Starr had kept a diary (which she called her Mem Book), and it was filled with highly erotic passages and descriptions of masochistic sexual trysts. No names were given but enough initials were there to keep newspaper gossips busy for a long while.

In recent times, as we shall learn later, Starr has been glamourously immortalized, in books and on the screen. But the depictions are inaccurate. In fact she was a sad creature driven by perversion nourished in her childhood into a compulsive life of sin and tragedy. The real story begins many years earlier and is little known. It is a shocking tale but true.

Starr's parents came from Boston and her mother was a distant relative of Andrew J. Peters. Peters, a former congressman and onetime mayor of Boston, was a wealthy and powerful man. He was also a man of few scruples.

One day while the young Starr was playing with Peters' children on the beach, she caught the older man's eye and sparked a per-

149

verted lust in him. As the weeks went by desire for her grew in him and finally he decided to act on it. Luring the eleven-year-old to a safe spot one afternoon, Peters produced a bottle of ether and forced sex on her. It must have been a provocative experience for him since he became so attached to Starr that he initiated a discreet but steady relationship with her that lasted on and off into her adulthood.

For a long time the illicit relationship went unnoticed by others, but it began to produce some very strange behavior in Starr for whom it was a devastatingly destructive experience. In the light of modern psychiatry it is understandable. To Starr's parents, not even knowing the cause, it was inexplicable.

Starr became obsessed with decency. She wore her dresses long when everyone else wore them around the knees. She never went swimming because she considered a swimsuit vulgar. She wore boys' clothing most of the time and continually sought out older people as associates. She also spent long periods alone, frequently locking herself in her room for days at a time to read philosophy and poetry.

In addition, she turned to drugs (which would always be a prerequisite to sex for her), she drank heavily, and she became an ether addict. When Starr was fifteen her mother divorced her first husband and married Stanley Faithfull. Both Starr and her younger sister Tucker quickly adopted their stepfather's last name. Stanley brought his new family to live in New York and Greenwich Village became Starr's new playground.

Starr's sex life expanded somewhat in her new home, but it remained a very twisted affair. Sex was very important for her but her traumatic early experiences prevented her from enjoying the act itself. She discovered that her real satisfaction came from teasing, from seeming to offer and then stretching out the sexual preliminaries as long as possible. Sometimes she gave in, other times she was simply taken by the aroused and angry man.

As her adolescent years passed, her Mem Book grew. Throughout this entire period she kept on seeing Peters—or AJP, as she called him. All the entries for AJP reflect the mixed emotions of fear, sickness, and attraction that kept her going.

Finally, after one particularly traumatic bout with AJP, Starr confessed her activities to her mother. The Faithfulls reacted by pressur-

150

Starr Faithfull. (UPI photo)

ing Peters with exposure and eventually a large sum of money (reportedly $80,000) was paid by "an unnamed individual" as a settlement.

Throughout this period Starr's parents spent large sums on various kinds of psychiatric care and counseling. None of it had much effect on her.

In 1930 Starr surfaced publicly for the first time in a midtown New York hotel. Hotel guests heard screams coming from her room and called the police. When a patrolman responding to the complaint opened the door he found Starr lying naked on the bed. A man, identified as Joseph Collins, was standing over her wearing only an undershirt. A bottle of gin stood on the night table. It was obvious that Collins had been beating her. The patrolman ordered him out (he disappeared very quickly) and sent Starr off to the hospital.

At Bellevue Hospital Starr claimed to be ignorant of what had happened. She blamed her lack of memory on drink. Hospital records show she was diagnosed as an alcoholic upon arrival and that she was treated for multiple contusions.

It is hardly surprising that neither the hospital nor the policeman made any more out of the incident. Unfortunately a number of men are sadists, who enjoy inflicting real or symbolic pain on women. Their tastes are satisfied by a special sort of prostitute who takes the beatings for money and by an equally strange sort of woman who actually enjoys pain and suffering.

While it is distinctly possible, even likely, that Starr was one of the latter, it seems probable since we know teasing was her favorite part of sex, that she got even greater satisfaction from the attraction-repulsion game she played. This doubtless arose in some way from the sexual trauma of her young years and may only incidentally have led to the beatings.

In Starr Faithfull's twenty-fifth year, the compulsive neuroses that gnawed at her life began to grow stronger and stronger. She traveled to London and promptly attempted suicide. Quick action saved her life, as twenty-four grains of allonal were pumped out of her stomach.

Back in New York, Starr discovered a new obsession, ships and farewells. She began to haunt the docks of Manhattan whenever the majestic ocean liners were preparing to leave. Dressed in her sharpest clothes and carrying a hip flash (her father disapproved of bathtub gin and always prepared a flask of martinis for her to carry), she would mingle with the passengers and well-wishers for the final minutes on board. She was usually drunk.

To any modern psychoanalyst her actions would have been clear and understandable, for the urgings to suicide were becoming more compelling within her. Leave-takings and the suggestion of last farewells they evoke, probably struck a very strong chord in Starr.

At one of these dockside revels—it was to be her last—she met a young Englishman, George Jameson-Carr. Jameson-Carr was a surgeon on board the 22,000-ton Cunard liner *Franconia*. Starr fell madly in love with the doctor at first sight. At first, Jameson-Carr may well have been unaware of Starr's compulsion, but her constant attentions created scenes he could hardly ignore.

Aware that something was amiss with the beautiful young woman and fearful for his position, Jameson-Carr did all he could to dissuade Starr from her blatant pursuit. Finally, as the ship was preparing to depart, he succeeded in getting her out of his sitting room. Starr did not leave the liner, however. Drunk, and torn by this new obsession and her old hateful urges, she stowed away. She was soon discovered and a very sorry scene ensued as she was put off, drunk, aboard an inbound tugboat.

Eleven days later an early morning stroller on Long Island found Starr's body washed up on the beach. The initial police autopsy showed that the body had been in the water for at least forty-eight hours. She had eaten a large meal and had taken a barbiturate prior to her death (enough to make her drowsy but not enough to kill her) and her lungs were full of sand. The upper part of her body was heavily bruised and she had been raped. This, coupled with the fact that she was dressed in a silk dress with no underclothes, led police to open a murder investigation.

At this point the story became front-page news. Clever reporting quickly unearthed much of Starr's bizarre past, which made for the kind of scandalous reading that city tabloid readers eat up. Hints of her sexual misadventures became the common thread in story after story. Starr's family added fuel to the flames by opening their house to the press and engaging in a great deal of speculation about her as well as exhibiting considerable eccentric behavior of their own.

Because of the controversy a second autopsy was performed, which indicated that the performance of sexual intercourse had been voluntary. Shortly after the autopsy the district attorney made a flamboyant announcement: "I know the identity of the two men who killed Starr Faithfull. One of them is a prominent New York politician. They took her to Long Beach, drugged her, and held her under the water until she was drowned. I will arrest both of them within thirty-six hours."

At this point George Jameson-Carr returned to New York on board the *Franconia*. Already aware of Starr's death, he immediately delivered to the authorities two letters written to him by Starr after the ship sailed. Both of them were about suicide. In the second Starr set out what she would do on her last day. Her plans included a good meal and a last flirtation.

The letters quickly ended the wide publicity given to the case. Both the public and the authorities accepted Starr's death as suicide. Although no one could quite explain all the circumstances, the investigation and the headlines ceased. No arrests were ever made.

Starr's story left the newspapers but for decades the intriguing and sensational nature of her life and death has continued to fascinate people. Two novels were based on her life and one of them, *Butterfield Eight,* by John O'Hara, became a popular movie. Starr's name is still well known to a surprising number of people.

What really happened to Starr Faithfull? The truth is buried forever in time, but several tantalizing facts remain to haunt us. It seems obvious that Starr did not kill herself. Drowning produces water in the lungs. The only explanation for sand in the lungs is murder. Someone must have held her head down in the shallow beach water, near the shore. Furthermore, the rest of Starr's clothes were never found, which seems highly unlikely if she was a suicide.

Did Starr pick up a new man and end her life in a masochistic scene on the beach? Did she choose a man she could taunt to violence as a way of committing suicide? Was her last night a final acting out of the trauma that plagued her since the age of eleven? And if so, how does one explain the voluntary sex that occurred

Starr's body as it was found on the beach.   (UPI photo)

before her death? Was she, by bizarre circumstance, abducted by a killer-rapist who was unaware of her mental state? No one will ever know. Starr Faithfull will remain forever an enigma on the pages of history.

Joseph Elwell

ONE OF THE MOST INTRIGUING MYSTERIES of the twentieth century ocurred during the euphoria that followed World War I. The victim in the case was Joseph Bowne Elwell, a man who lived high and who had impeccable taste. In 1920 Elwell was one of the world's leading experts on auction bridge. He was also one of the richest.

By the age of forty he had developed a skill with cards and a kind of natural class that enabled him to play high-stake bridge with some of the wealthiest people of the day. Games of ten dollars a point were common and on some nights he took home as much as $30,000.

He also taught bridge and by doing so picked up the tidy sum of $18,000 a year (remember, these are 1920 dollars). Several years earlier he had written a definitive book on bridge, the sales of which earned him an additional $7,500 per annum.

Elwell believed in living well. Home was a four-story granite mansion on Manhattan's West Side. When he tired of the city he had a choice of three vacation homes, one each in Newport, Southampton (Long Island), and Palm Beach. He drove around in a chauffeured $7,000 limousine. He also owned a yacht and a stable of racing thoroughbreds in Kentucky.

Elwell had another love besides bridge, and that was women. Between bridge games and trips to his houses, he managed to see a wide variety of women from some of New York's most fashionable circles. He had so many that ultimately he was forced to keep a card index. It was a card index that was to become very famous.

On Friday morning, June 11, 1920, Elwell's housekeeper, Marie Larsen, arrived at his Manhattan town house. She was moving

157

Joseph Elwell as bon vivant.   (UPI photo)

slowly. It was only 8:15 A.M. and it already was hot. She wasn't looking forward to the extreme heat the afternoon would bring.

Mrs. Larsen opened the massive front doors and began the task of cleaning the residence. She started in the kitchen and slowly worked her way around the first floor. She was in no hurry. No one was expected before noon and there was no sign of the master. He often slept late.

When Mrs. Larsen got to the reception room she noticed several letters scattered on the floor. Absentmindedly she stooped to pick them up. As she did so her attention turned up to the chair in front of her and she screamed. There, just a feet away, sat her master, Joseph Elwell, his face blackened and coverd with blood.

At first Mrs. Larsen thought he was dead, but after watching for a few moments she realized that he was still breathing. For a second she hesitated between her fright and her protective instincts as a housekeeper. Elwell was dressed in his pajamas and was without his toupee and false teeth—a self he never let outsiders see. Then panic took hold and Mrs. Larsen dashed outside and grabbed the first people she could find.

These turned out to be the milkman and the local policeman. Mrs. Larsen hurried them inside, mumbling something about Mr. Elwell being "sick."

The policeman laid the "illness" theory to rest after one look at Elwell. There was a hole in his forehead and the black stuff around the hole was gunpowder. "This guy's been shot," the policeman announced and promptly called homicide and an ambulance.

Among the earliest arrivals at the house was Dr. Charles Norris, the medical examiner. Dr. Norris lived a few blocks away and walked over when he heard about the incident. Aided by a detective the examiner made a preliminary search of the house. One of the first things he noticed was the absence of a gun. Mrs. Larsen assured everybody that she had touched nothing and had not seen a gun.

Norris took a careful look around the reception room. Two cigarettes were found, one on the rug and one on the mantel. The telephone was broken. In one wall large cracks signaled the spot where a bullet had lodged itself. The trajectory indicated it was the same bullet that had pierced Elwell's head.

A check of all the entrances and windows revealed that everything was locked from the inside except for a window on the third floor. The windows were further protected by iron grills.

A short time later Norris was notified that Elwell had died at the hospital. At that point the police suspected the murder weapon was a 45-caliber handgun.

Norris determined that Elwell had not committed suicide. There were thirty-four powder marks on the victim's face, the medical examiner added, indicating the weapon had been fired from a distance of at least three feet, possibly four. Norris also stated that the exit hole in the back of the skull was higher than the entrance hole in the front. This would mean a shot fired from the waist or a crouched position.

By now homicide detectives had begun a thorough search of the townhouse. They found a shell casing under Elwell's chair and pried the slug out of the wall. Both came from a 45-caliber gun.

Each of the letters on the floor was read. They all proved to be innocuous. It appeared that Elwell had picked up the mail after the morning delivery and had sat down in the reception room to read them when he was shot. This further destroyed any attempt to write the death off as a suicide. Reading the morning mail is hardly the last act of a man about to kill himself.

The policemen went through the second and third floors, mixing detective work with awe. In 1920 a cop rarely found himself amid the kind of luxury and art that made up Joseph Elwell's world. In the master bedroom the detectives found the dead man's toupee, along with some expensive cuff links and $400 in cash. Clearly, robbery had not been the motive.

In another room a woman's bed jacket was found. Embroidered initials on the jacket had been cut off. When asked about the jacket Mrs. Larsen replied, "I wouldn't know. Mr. Elwell is separated from his wife." Police quickly learned that Elwell had a fifteen-year-old son as well, but that neither wife nor child were part of his life or likely suspects. Mrs. Elwell, who had helped him with the bridge book that started his climb to wealth, had left him because of his countless affairs with other women.

The first of those women was heard from at lunchtime when Florence Ellenson called from Asbury Park. Florence was "very

160

Medical examiner Charles Norris—he said he knew who killed Elwell, but he never told.   (UPI photo)

upset" because Elwell had failed to show up for their luncheon date. She added that Elwell had phoned her at eight that morning.

As the police continued to search, they came up with the famous card index. On it were the names of more than fifty women, a lot of them well known. Ordinarily the police might have handled the index discretely, but Elwell was a person of some reputation and his death was rapidly becoming a nationwide story. As a result the police began a careful check of all the women on the index.

They also began to reconstruct Elwell's last night and as they did so a lot of very interesting names began to turn up. That fateful evening the bridge expert had dined at the Ritz-Carlton with financier Walter Lewisohn. At the party had been one of Elwell's friends, Mrs. Lewisohn's sister, Viola Kraus, for whom the dinner had been a kind of celebration. Earlier in the day she had secured her divorce from playboy Victor von Schlegel. Von Schlegel, apparently to no one's surprise, had turned up at the Ritz-Carlton with an attractive woman dressed in a black evening gown.

After dinner Elwell's party went dancing at the top of the hotel. Von Schlegel and his partner followed them up. As this story leaked to the press (and just about everything about it did), the public ate it up. This vicarious peek into the lives of the wealthy made for exciting reading. Von Schlegel's unnamed companion was quickly labeled "the woman in black." The newspapers immediately began a quest to identify her.

After leaving the Ritz-Carlton, Elwell and his friends went to the top of the Amsterdam Hotel for a floor show, more champagne, and dancing. At this point Elwell and Viola had a fight. At 1:30 A.M. Elwell excused himself and left the hotel alone.

At this point the story becomes confusing. Despite intensive efforts, the police were never able to unravel the conflicting reports of what happened next. A cab driver reported that he picked up Elwell at the Amsterdam Hotel at 1:45 A.M. and took him to his home, pausing only to get a copy of the *Morning Telegraph* for his passenger. A copy of the paper was found on the victim's bed.

Other witnesses said they saw Elwell walk to the Café Montmartre on Broadway. There he allegedly got into a conversation with two men and a woman and accepted their invitation for a lift home in their noisy roadster. Neighbors testified that they had seen such a car parked in front of Elwell's house at 3:45 A.M. No one was seen entering or leaving.

To further confuse the issue, Viola claimed that she had called Elwell at 1:45 A.M. to apoligize for the spat. Telephone records also indicated that a call was placed from Elwell's phone at 4:30 A.M. to a

Elwell's wife, Helen Derby.   (UPI photo)

friend of his on Long Island. The friend denied ever receiving such a call.

Another cabby approached police and said he, too, had made a late-night trip to the Elwell residence. This cabby said his passengers were a man and a woman and that they arrived about 6 A.M. The driver said he was told to wait while the two went into the townhouse. A short time later he heard a scream from inside and fled. The authorities discounted this story.

With these trails ending in confusion the police redoubled their efforts to track down Elwell's women. Many of those on the index turned out to be former "friends." Many of them said they had relatives or male friends who might have had it in for Elwell, but an extensive check provided every suspect with an alibi.

Others on the list were still active in the bridge expert's romantic life. Many of these were receiving small monthly sums from Elwell—"love pensions," as the press called them.

At this point police discovered a bundle of women's nightclothes in the basement. They were quickly identified as belonging to Viola Kraus. A very red-faced housekeeper admitted that she had hid the clothing shortly after the murder. Mrs. Larsen had a very strong sense of propriety.

Police quickly returned their attention to Viola's former husband, Von Schlegel. In order to provide himself with an alibi he was forced to identify the "woman in black" who had accompanied him that fateful night. By this time the Elwell case was front page news and the information that Von Schlegel had the woman ensconced in a hotel suite which adjoined his kept housewives tut-tutting for days.

As the significant leads began to evaporate the harried police grasped more and more at straws. Rumors and anonymous tips began to pour in from a titilated public. Although these tips produced scandalous newspaper stories, they brought the authorities no closer to a solution.

In the end, as the months passed and no further clues were uncovered, the investigation faltered, and finally, for all practical purposes, stopped. The district attorney's office declared that despite one of the most massive murder investigations in New York's history, the authorities were left with nothing more than suspicions. Rumors flew, implicating a high unnamed city official in the death. Elwell's mother claimed that the killer was known but considered untouchable. Dr. Norris, the medical examiner, said he knew who did it, but he carried his secret to the grave.

A final twist occurred a year after the murder. At that point two men and a woman showed up at the Elwell townhouse, which had been put up for sale. They were taken around the place by the caretaker. The tour was brief and the strangers seemed interested only in Elwell's bedroom. One of the men stepped forward and tapped the walls and floor of the bedroom closet. "It's hollow sure enough," were his only words. With that the group left.

A week later the woman returned alone. Slipping the caretaker five dollars she went up to the bedroom by herself. A few minutes later she quickly left the house carrying something under her cape.

With that the case moved into the realm of mystery magazines and history. It is a story filled with conflicting facts, mysterious suspects, and unknown motives. To this day no one knows who really killed Joseph Bowne Elwell. No one may ever know.

WHERE ARE THEY?

Every year thousands of people disappear. Some walk out of boring lives. Others flee from emotional problems. Very rarely are any of these people famous. It's simply too hard to vanish when you are well known. When somebody famous manages to pull it off, it creates a public mystery of the first order.

What Ever Happened to Judge Crater?

ON AUGUST 6, 1930, one of the greatest mysteries in modern American history began. On that evening newly appointed New York State Supreme Court Justice Joseph Force Crater dined in a fancy Broadway restaurant with theatrical lawyer William Klein and a sexy actress named Sally-Lou Ritz. The dinner was ordinary in all respects. Only the ending was unusual. Finishing his coffee, the six-foot, 190-pound judge rose and bid his friends farewell. He was, he said, off to the theater. It was 9:15. He walked out the front door of the restaurant, hailed a cab, and was never seen again.

Judge Crater was no ordinary man. He was a member of the Empire State's second highest court, and an important cog in the Tammany Hall machine, a public figure, and a "solid member of the community." He spoke and appeared constantly at gatherings and was a popular figure at famous restaurants and clubs across the city. His face was known to thousands. It is not easy for such a man simply to disappear. But Judge Crater did just that, vanishing from the earth more completely than any other prominent American in recent history.

In the months and years that followed his disappearance, countless investigations were undertaken by everyone from the city and state police to newspapers and private detectives. Rewards were offered and even a clairvoyant was called in. The official search for the justice in 1930–31 alone cost more than $250,000. Despite all this not one solid clue to what really happened has ever been discovered. This massive search has unearthed only dramatic hints of mystery and a picture of Judge Crater that varies drastically from the image of uprightness that existed before his disappearance.

Tall and portly, the white-haired jurist looked every bit the picture of a movie judge. He was impeccably dressed and constantly maintained a solemnity that led many to believe him a wise and honest man. He was tall and he had a presence that affected everyone around him.

It turned out, however, that these were only superficial characteristics. Crater owed his position and steady advancement entirely to his connections with Tammany Hall. In Democratic clubs all across the city he was known as "good old Joe," always ready with a quick handshake and a racy story.

Good old Joe also liked another kind of club, the kind that offered illegal whiskey and easy women. Although he lived in a fashionable Fifth Avenue apartment and summered in Bar Harbor, Maine, with his elegant wife, Stella, he greatly preferred a weekend of speakeasies and loose women. On more than one occasion the supreme court justice whiled away the weekend at Atlantic City, together with a few of his cronies and a lot of "all-night women."

Crater's favorite hangout was a Broadway speakeasy called the Club Abbey. It was a strange place for a supreme court justice. The Abbey was owned by gang lord Owney Madden and it was a notorious meeting place for corrupt politicians and underworld kingpins. The Abbey's clients included such figures as Jack "Legs" Diamond, Dutch Schultz, Vincent "Mad Dog" Coll, and Vivian Gordon. Crater assumed the name of Joe Crane when visiting the Abbey, but considering the number of politicians and judges in the place it is highly unlikely that anyone failed to know who he really was.

Crater had only been a supreme court justice for a short time when he disappeared. His was an interim appointment meant as a political compromise and he was by no means sure of winning the upcoming election (New York state elects its supreme court justices). Before that he had risen slowly but steadily through the political machine that owned New York City during Prohibition days.

Crater started out as a young lawyer in Pennsylvania. He was known as bright and fun loving. When he came to New York and joined the local Democratic club he quickly found himself in his

Judge Crater, where are you? (UPI photo)

element. He was a hard worker and knew how, when, and with whom to ingratiate himself. Local politicos were impressed with his natural ability to navigate in the turbulent waters of big-city politics.

Crater began working for Justice Robert Wagner and teaching law at night, all the while building up a growing private practice. At the same time he established a solid network of acquaintances in the all-important Democratic wards.

In 1917 Crater met and married one of his clients, stylish Stella Mance Wheeler. The new Mrs. Crater seemed to be the final touch for the rising young lawyer-politician and within a few years he acquired his first judgeship. The Craters' standard of living increased at the same time and although they never lived as lavishly as many, their lives were a great deal more than comfortable.

Judge Crater's appointment to one of the state's highest courts came at a critical point in his life. During the preceding two years a wave of corruption investigations had swept the country as a whole, and especially New York City, and in their wake had toppled a large number of politicians and judges. During this same period Crater had apparently become a party to a large fraud involving city funds. At one point he commented to his wife, "If they'll just leave us alone for five or six years, we'll make a lot of money." At the same time it is highly probable that Crater had become involved in the sale of judgeships—first by buying his own and then through patronage. He was also linked to one of the biggest corruption cases exposed at the time. Although he was never indicted, it was a time of great uncertainty for him.

This was the atmosphere and background that Judge Crater carried with him when he and his wife left for Bar Harbor in June of 1930. In July he made a short trip to New York to deal with the city fraud case. He also made a side trip to Atlantic City for what was later labeled by the press "an all-night whoopee party" with three women.

Crater returned to Maine on August 1 but the next day his vacation was interrupted by a tense phone call from New York. Mrs. Crater remembers the call as being short, and angry, with the judge saying little more than "yes," "go on," and "I understand." When he hung up the judge muttered to himself, "I've got to straighten those fellows out.'' With that he informed his wife that he had to return to New York at once. Assuring her that he would be back by the eighth, he left on August 3 for the city.

When Judge Crater arrived in New York he proceeded directly to his Fifth Avenue apartment and told the maid to take a four-day vacation. For the next two days he led what seemed to be a normal life, working in his office and meeting with peers.

On the morning of the sixth Crater was visited in his office by Simon Rifkind. Rifkind was a close friend of Crater's and a very high-priced lawyer. No one knows to this day what they talked about, but when Rifkind left, Crater wrote out two checks totaling $5,100 and sent one of his assistants off to cash them. As soon as the assistant was gone Crater began to sort through his personal files, pulling out large numbers of papers. He filled his briefcase with these and then used the briefcase of another assistant as well as four large legal portfolios for the rest. When the first assistant returned with the money, Crater slipped it in his pocket without counting it, picked up the papers, and left for his apartment.

What the papers were or what Crater did with them has remained a mystery. They were gone when Crater's apartment was searched later and there was no sign that they had been burned or shredded. No one in or near the building ever saw them carried out.

Around dinner time Crater turned up at a Broadway ticket office and reserved one seat for that evening's performance of a hit play. Shortly after that he arrived at the Broadway restaurant where he met William Klein and the showgirl and where he passed from being a state judge to being a national mystery.

The first person to miss him was his wife. When August 9 came and went without his return she began to worry. Not only was her husband dependable about his schedule, but he was also considerate and always called ahead if his plans changed.

Mrs. Crater waited six days before inquiring, on the assumption that any accident would be reported in the papers. When nothing happened she sent the chauffeur into New York to investigate. He found nothing to explain the disappearance. All of Crater's cronies, however, insisted that there was nothing to be worried about. But when the judge's court sessions resumed and he still hadn't shown up, Mrs. Crater began contacting friends. A police investigation was begun and within weeks the story leaked out and became front-page news.

After that, things moved fast. New York governor Franklin Roosevelt (facing an election himself) ordered a state investigation. New York City mayor Jimmy Walker put up a $5,000 reward.

At first the investigation was promising. The judge's assistant first denied cashing the checks and then another checking account was discovered. But these leads petered out and the investigation stalled. Having nothing else to go on, the police tackled the judge's private life. They very quickly traced the women in Atlantic City and found out about the many raucous nights in the Abbey Club. Before too long, they also turned up a full-time mistress in New York.

The woman's name was Connie Marcus. A modish woman in her thirties, she was energetic and attractive. Connie told the police she had become involved with the judge when he handled her divorce proceedings. They had started an affair that continued for years. Crater saw her several times a week and helped pay her rent. Despite all this, Connie Marcus proved no help at all in locating her lover.

As all of these details (which were extremely lurid in 1930) became known, the story spread across the country. The depression was a year old and with alcohol still illegal the public was hungry for titillation. Enterprising journalists interviewed everyone who had anything to do with the case. Although their work uncovered virtually nothing new, it succeeded in fanning interest in the case to a fever pitch.

As the investigation began to grind to a halt the police became more and more desperate. Detectives were sent to investigate all sorts of tenuous leads in different parts of the country. Plans were made to drag a lake in Maine. Mrs. Crater received a ransom note, but the police had quickly proved it a forgery. A grand jury was convened but it had access to no more information than did anyone else. On November 7 it issued a statement saying it had learned nothing about what had happened to Judge Crater.

There the matter rested until late in January of 1931 when Mrs. Crater announced that she had found a large manila envelope containing $6,690 in a bureau drawer. Also in the drawer were three

Judge Crater's wife holding the mystery list that was "found" after his disappearance.   (UPI photo)

checks endorsed by the judge, a pile of stocks and bonds, three life-insurance policies, and a handwritten list of people who owed the judge money. The list was signed, "I am very whary, Joe."

Mrs. Crater's discovery caused an uproar. The police had searched the apartment several times as part of the investigation and swore that it was inconceivable that they could have missed the envelope. "It is so fantastic as to be suspicious," said a high police official.

Despite massive speculation and a renewed investigation no one ever determined how the envelope got there (or whether Mrs. Crater brought it from Maine). This was the last dramatic development in the case. Slowly the newspapers let the story die, but for years the judge's disappearance was a topic of national debate. Stand-up comedians used the judge in their routines. Sensation seekers reported seeing the judge in different countries. To this day "What ever happened to Judge Crater?" is a catch phrase for millions of Americans old enough to remember the headlines.

What did happen to Judge Crater? Nothing more than an educated guess is possible. There are several theories from among which you can take your pick.

Many high-placed sources felt that the judge was murdered trying to cross one of his associates in corruption. Some said Crater had refused to make an alleged $22,500 additional payoff for his judgeship. Others said he had tried to cut a major underworld figure out of a illegal scheme of some sort. In the world of 1930 New York, this kind of motive would have been sufficient to kill, even someone as prominent as Crater. People like Al Capone and Dutch Schultz ordered executions regularly on less provocation. The major stumbling block to this theory is the lack of any really sizable amount of cash in any of the judge's bank accounts. If this was the motive, where did the hot money go? Or was the judge murdered before he could collect? No one will ever know.

A more bizarre theory was set forth by the *New York Daily Mirror*. The *Mirror* claimed that Judge Crater had become disillusioned by his corrupt life and had sought solace in Catholicism. According to the newspaper Crater had had a soulful session with Connie Marcus and then left to enter a monastery in Mexico.

This theory was matched in its bizarreness by that in a competing tabloid, where the judge's death was laid to a night of excess in a local whorehouse. According to this account the judge died in the act and was disposed of by the underworld to avoid publicity.

The most interesting speculation, however, was put forth by the *Daily News.*

The *News* developed a source linking Crater to a well-known Brooklyn man convicted of mortgage fraud (the judge was said to have offered to fix the case). A little digging disclosed that the lawyer for the Brooklyn man was also the lawyer and lover of Vivian Gordon, the merciless blackmailer and supplier of call girls, who was, in turn, as we have already seen, a regular member of the Abbey Club.

One of Vivian's enforcers, Harry Stein, testified that he had met Crater in Vivian's apartment. Was Vivian blackmailing Judge Crater? Had one of her girls taken incriminating photos of him? Was she threatening Crater with previews of her upcoming testimony? Harry Stein and the other enforcer, Chowderhead Cohen, were violent men. Did they try to rough up the judge and killed him in the process?

The final chapter in the Crater disappearance came in 1959 when *Harper's* magazine hired a Dutch clairvoyant to solve the case. The clairvoyant quickly opened a trail that led to a retired New York butcher named Krauss. Krauss had been a member of the Tammany machine and knew Crater and the other prominent figures of the day. He also maintained a house in Yonkers which he made available to machine members for "parties and deals." Krauss stated he had heard rumors that Crater and others had made $90,000 on a "deal" and had buried the money in the Yonkers backyard.

The next time Krauss visited the house he found blood splattered in the kitchen and a gaping hole in the rose garden. A bit later he was told, "Crater's dead. He's buried up there." The clairvoyant determined the exact site of the body but when the magazine people dug, nothing was found.

As you read this, the Judge Crater case remains a mystery to the police and the public. What little chance of being solved the case ever had dwindles as the people surrounding the disappearance die off. What is left is a national enigma that still causes comment whenever the subject of missing persons is brought up. As late as 1960 the judge was used as a character in the hit musical *Fiorello*. What ever did happen to Judge Crater? No one will ever know.

Lord Lucan

BELGRAVIA IS AN ELEGANT, upper-class section of London. Throughout Great Britain's rise to empire and in the years since, a solid phalanx of titled peers has inhabited the area and bestowed on it a special quality of "respectability" that has kept it from many of the less elegant encroachments of modern society. It is a neighborhood of enforced leisure, of backgammon and high-stake card games, of private clubs, and of repressed emotions and face saved at any cost.

Troubles have come to various members of this elite group through the years, but the solidarity of the upper class and the determination of its members to maintain their image has usually kept these imbroglios from public view. But on November 7, 1975, tragedy struck in Belgravia and left an imprint that could not, no matter how great the effort, be covered up.

On that fateful day, Richard John Bingham, the seventh earl of Lucan and a peer of the realm, apparently murdered his children's nanny, brutally attacked his wife with a piece of lead pipe, and then disappeared so totally that the combined efforts of Scotland Yard, a variety of national agencies, and even foreign police departments have been unable to find a trace of him. In the years since, hundreds of detectives, reporters, and writers have struggled to find the truth behind these bizarre and bloody events but so far no one has succeeded.

To many people Lord Lucan (nicknamed Lucky Lucan by his friends!) was the quintessence of the upper class. Born into an old noble family, he moved from his earliest years in an atmosphere of wealth, status, and snobbism. Despite the fact that his mother and

181

father were Socialists and renegades against upper-class respectability (though not renegades enough to give up their life-style), he burrowed his way deep into the more conventional kind of life led by his peers. He attended Eton and became an officer in the Coldstream Guards. He maintained a lavish home in London and belonged to the Clermont, the most prestigious gambling club in town. He did not work in any normal sense of the word and his daily routine centered around meals and gambling at the club.

Most of what has been written about Lord Lucan, the man, has come from information provided by the people he knew, generally people with a stake in protecting his (and their) image. He is described by them as a person to be emulated, a leader of men, and an aristocrat dedicated to loyalty, honesty, and reliability. He was said to be the perfect husband, patient and understanding, and the ideal social companion as well. His style was impeccable, and in the world he traveled in, style was most important of all. Occasionally, however facts have slipped out which paint a far different picture than that given above.

Some who knew him considered Lucky to be a highly repressed and boring man whose chief interest lay in being terribly upper class. His schedule was so predictable that he not only ate every meal at the same establishment but ordered the same dish every day. At home he had a huge wardrobe of identical custom-made pinstripe suits. On his bookshelves he kept a collection of Hitler's speeches along with books on mental illness. He didn't like to talk to people who weren't wearing proper shoelaces and didn't seem to like women or sex at all. One of his biggest personal traumas was the fact that his great-great-grandfather had ordered the Charge of the Light Brigade, a horrendous military blunder in the Crimean War.

This, then, was the man who in 1963 married Veronica Duncan, the daughter of an army major, and tried to start a family. From the very beginning the marriage seemed doomed.

Veronica was the youngest of two middle-class daughters raised by a hotelkeeper after the death of their father. Her older sister was tall, attractive, and popular and because Veronica lived constantly in her shadow, she suffered from an enormous inferiority complex. Then the sister married a millionaire from Lucan's circle of associates.

Lord and Lady Lucan before the split. (UPI photo)

No one seems to quite know why Lord Lucan married Veronica (probably because it was "time" to take a wife and she was at hand) but everyone is sure why Veronica did it. "Elevation" is how she puts it. "A chance to be someone" is how others put it.

Veronica obviously had strong ideas about what her new title would bring her. Dinners with important people, exciting balls lasting until morning, the opportunity to hobnob with royalty—these are the kinds of things that seemed to fill her mind. What she found was something else altogether.

Lord Lucan was not an important man. He was also deeply tied to a very conservative, male-dominated society that was almost the exact opposite of what Veronica imagined. In Lucan's world the wife was expected to live her own life and accept her role of silent, noninterfering partner. Lord Lucan spent the majority of his time "with the boys." He didn't expect marriage to change that.

Not only did Veronica have dreams about upper-class life, she was also impatient, highly intelligent, and very sharp-tongued. For Lucky Lucan, the combination was a disaster.

At the very beginning, they led a tranquil life. Everything around Veronica was new to her and required some getting used to. She had to redecorate the house in Belgravia, the right furnishings had to be chosen. She had a whole new wardrobe to buy and a long list of people to learn about.

In time, however, Veronica came to realize that marriage to Lucan wasn't about to bring her the kind of life she'd expected. There were no fancy balls, no meetings with the Queen, and at the dinners the men treated her like a piece of furniture.

Veronica gave vent to her frustration by using the only weapon she had—her corrosive tongue. She quickly became known as a woman who didn't know her place. Middle class by background, she had no sense of the proprieties of the upper class. Her gaffes were frequent. The fact that she was obviously more intelligent than her husband didn't help either.

As she became more and more isolated from her husband and his friends, who were blacklisting her socially, she decided that her only possible course was to force herself back into his world. She began to dine with Lord Lucan every night at his club despite the fact that he virtually ignored her. Regularly ostracized, she stood bitterly around the Clermont, night after night, gradually withdrawing into loneliness and paranoia. This situation lasted almost nine years.

By the beginning of 1973 the constant tension between the two reached a breaking point. Lord Lucan walked out and demanded custody of his children (three by this time, including a male heir). Veronica fought back and the legal-emotional battle began.

Lord Lucan hoped to pressure and humiliate Veronica into submission. He had already twice tried to have her committed and during the past year had taken to wearing a concealed microphone and recording their conversations. Now he hired detectives to follow her around day and night and began making harassing anonymous phone calls.

In March, Lucan got a court order for temporary custody of his children and promptly kidnapped two of them. They seemed to have become the focal point of his life now. As one friend put it, "after the tragedy of the Light Brigade . . . they were his hope for the future."

In June, Veronica won the court battle and regained custody of the children. Lord Lucan began to deteriorate rapidly. He became a chain smoker and drank constantly. He became a nuisance, cornering friends and talking endlessly about his children. At the same time his gambling skills deteriorated and his already shaky financial state became worse.

On the day of the crime there was little in Lord Lucan's behavior to indicate what was to come. Only a discerning eye would have noticed that one of his many visits was to a pharmacy to ask about a pill his wife was taking or that after inviting four friends to eat with him he made only four reservations for dinner.

At the house in Belgravia it was the nanny's night off. Sandra Rivett had only been with the family for four weeks. Because of household pressures and Lady Lucan's state of mind there had been a steady turnover of nursemaids. During the afternoon Sandra came down with a cold and decided to remain at the house overnight. It was a fatal decision.

While Lord Lucan's dinner guests were making themselves comfortable at his club and wondering at his absence, Lucky was stealthily entering his Belgravia home (Lady Lucan was the only

185

witness to the happenings and the description of the attack is based on her account plus the assumptions made about it by Scotland Yard). Hefting a heavy iron pipe Lord Lucan waited for his wife to appear. Thinking her to be the only woman in the house, he never doubted that it was she who was the form in front of him in the darkness. Without warning he brutally beat her with the pipe, causing her to fall to the bottom of the basement stairs. The assault was terrible. The nanny never had a chance.

In all probability Lord Lucan did not realize his mistake until Lady Lucan appeared screaming on the staircase. Still wielding the pipe he returned to the attack, but Veronica turned out to be a tough customer. Actually pulling part of the railing away in her struggle, she managed to get out of the house before he killed her. Dripping blood and screaming for help, she ran down the street to a nearby establishment. In the meantime, Lucky Lucan stuffed the unfortunate nanny into a mail sack and left her in the basement before fleeing in a borrowed car.

Police responded to the alarm in minutes and the entire area surrounding the house soon became a madhouse of police, reporters, and gawkers. For three days Scotland Yard studied the evidence. Then they obtained a warrant for Lord Lucan. The charge: murder and attempted murder.

Lord Lucan's initial behavior after the attacks was that of a temporarily deranged man. He sought friends (he was unable to find them), and then began traveling away from London in an apparently random manner. He finally stopped at the home of a friend some distance away and wrote three rambling letters proclaiming his innocence. With that he left the house and disappeared forever.

The police hunted for him diligently but they were severely hampered by the attitudes of his friends and associates. Almost to a man (and a woman) they refused to cooperate. All of them looked on Lord Lucan as a terribly wronged man driven to whatever strange acts by the sadism of his distinctly middle-class wife. They also looked on the police as even worse than middle class. Not only did the people who knew the facts refuse to cooperate, many of them went so far as to advise others to hide things. To this day the police are sure that some of Lucan's associates know precisely what happened.

The story of the Belgravia murder made front-page news all across England. To have a peer of the realm be a murderer was heady stuff. People rushed to the newsstands to read whatever they could about it. For most of the English the world of Lord Lucan is a closed preserve, never open to public view. As its sordid details continued to come to light, the case gained a notoriety far in excess of the importance of the crime itself. The story became steady feature material and the scandal quickly spread to papers across Europe and the U.S.

Shortly after the crime, Lucan's closest associates held a private meeting to decide how to deal with the situation. Their primary goal apparently was how to help him.

It may well have been this group that abetted Lord Lucan's disappearance. With the power and connections of the aristocracy, it wouldn't have been difficult to get him quietly out of the country. It also seems highly likely that someone among his friends arranged for the transfer of funds adequate to his needs.

To this day no one outside this circle has any idea where the errant lord is. Rumors abound. Most of them suggest he is living in Europe—Spain and Portugal are often hinted at—under an alias. Still others say he is alive and well, hidden at the Clermont itself.

Scotland Yard, along with England's other investigative and im-migration services, have worked hard to find him. Countless inquiries and descriptions have been sent to other countries. Hundreds upon hundreds of investigative man-hours have been spent on the case. Still no clue has appeared. Where is Lord Lucan? Is he in fact alive? No one knows. No one may ever know.

Bibliography

For more reading . . . about the cases in this book and other fascinating unsolved mysteries, we recommend the following:

- *Guilty or Not Guilty* by William Greenwood. Hutchison & Co., Ltd., 1931.
- *Murders Most Strange* by Leonard Gribble. J. Long, 1959.
- *Murders Not Quite Solved* by Alvin Harloe J. Messur, Inc., 1938.
- *The Minister and the Choir Singer* by William Kunstler. Morrow, 1964.
- *Great Murder Mysteries* by Guy Logan. S. Pauls Co., 1931.
- *Butcher's Dozen and Other Murders* by John Martin. Harper & Row, 1950.
- *Murder by Witchcraft* by Donald McCormick. J. Long, 1968.
- *The Bizarre and the Bloody* by David Mellwain. Hart Publishing Co., 1972.
- *The Murderer's Companion* by Wilber Roughead. The Press of the Reader's Club, 1941.
- *The Anatomy of Murder* by Helen Simpson. The Macmillan Co., 1934.
- *Murder in New Orleans* by Robert Tallant. William Kimber, 1952.
- *Blood and Money* by Thomas Thompson. Doubleday & Co., Inc., 1976.
- *The Encyclopedia of Murder* by Colin Wilson and Patricia Pitman. Putnam, 1961.